TRUE
TALES
OF
ANGEL
ENCOUNTERS

To Write to the Author

If you wish to contact the author or would like more information about this book, please write to the author in care of Llewellyn Worldwide and we will forward your request. Both the author and publisher appreciate hearing from you and learning of your enjoyment of this book and how it has helped you. Llewellyn Worldwide cannot guarantee that every letter written to the author can be answered, but all will be forwarded. Please write to:

Carmel Reilly
c/o Llewellyn Worldwide
2143 Wooddale Drive, Dept. 978-0-7387-1494-3
Woodbury, MN 55125-2989, U.S.A.

Please enclose a self-addressed stamped envelope for reply,
or $1.00 to cover costs. If outside U.S.A., enclose
international postal reply coupon.

Many of Llewellyn's authors have websites with additional information and resources. For more information, please visit our website at:

www.llewellyn.com

TRUE TALES OF ANGEL ENCOUNTERS

Carmel Reilly

Llewellyn Publications
Woodbury, Minnesota

Published in 2009 by Llewellyn Publications.

First Llewellyn Edition
First Printing, 2009

Cover design by Lisa Novak
Cover image © Corbis/SuperStock

Llewellyn is a registered trademark of Llewellyn Worldwide, Ltd.

Library of Congress Cataloging-in-Publication Data
True tales of angel encounters / [edited by] Carmel Reilly. — 1st Llewellyn ed.
    p.   cm.
 ISBN 978-0-7387-1494-3
 1. Angels—Miscellanea. I. Reilly, Carmel.
 BF1999.T69 2009
 202'.15—dc22

                  2009002841

Llewellyn Publications
A Division of Llewellyn Worldwide, Ltd.
2143 Wooddale Drive, Dept. 978-0-7387-1494-3
Woodbury, MN 55125-2989, U.S.A.
www.llewellyn.com

Printed in the United States of America

CONTENTS

INTRODUCTION

I have always been fascinated by angels, ever since I was very young. Several times, as a child, I had encounters with spiritual beings, and ever since I have been certain that there are angels around us in the world.

Last year, as part of my ongoing research into the spiritual realm, I took out advertisements in a wide variety of publications and forums, asking people to send me accounts of their personal meetings with angels. Most such appeals produce an enthusiastic response, but in this case the number of communications I received was simply overwhelming. I had thousands of e-mails, faxes, and letters with all kinds of stories and memories from people around the world. A large number of the accounts included here are taken from personal interviews or telephone conversations in which individuals gave me more detail about their experiences.

As well as showing how strong the interest and belief in angels is, this fascinating experience reinforced my conviction that such a belief—one that cuts across all creeds and ages—cannot be without foundation. All the major religions include accounts of higher spiritual beings—what I refer to here as angels. The Christian church considers angels as both divine messengers and part of the heavenly host. Judaism, Islam, Buddhism, and Hinduism have their interpretations of angels. It is even more remarkable to observe that even the non-religious often believe in angels. The idea of angels is by no means restricted to those who have a firm religious faith or even a religious upbringing.

Accounts of angels go far back into antiquity. They are referred to in the earliest books of the Bible, and also in the most ancient scriptures of other religions. I'm not certain that we can ever know all there is to know about these mysterious beings, so it seems presumptuous to claim any knowledge that goes beyond mortal limits. However, I do believe that by comparing and contrasting the wide variety of historical sources, we can come up with a reasonably accurate picture of what angels are and how they relate to people. In this book, I'll share some firsthand accounts of angels, loosely arranged by subject. I'll also comment on the stories and speculate on what we can learn about angels.

The accounts in this book are taken almost verbatim from the messages I received in the course of my research. Only minor changes have been made. My editors have standardized spelling and grammar, and broken the stories into paragraphs where necessary, especially where I've taken the words from transcriptions of interviews rather than from letters or e-mails. In some cases, I've edited the stories down to a more compact length, but I have tried not to make any cuts or alterations that would materially affect the substance of what I was told.

It hasn't been easy to decide which of the accounts I received to include here, or how to categorize them. In the end, my decisions were made mainly on the grounds that I wanted to incorporate as wide a variety of experiences as possible. The chapters are organized around the ways that angels interact with us, starting with angels in times of crisis, everyday angels, healing angels, angels that intervene,, guardian angels, and messenger angels.

There seems to be a slight difference between what happens when angels heal us and when they bring us messages, for example, so I have separated these into their own sections. This should not be taken to reflect any fundamental distinction between healing angels and messenger angels; the accounts are simply grouped by the angles' actions. There are, of course, some accounts that could have been grouped differently. In such cases, I made the decision based on what I felt was most remarkable and distinctive about the encounter.

Because of space considerations, I wasn't able to include every story; in particular, I had a large number of reports of guardian angels helping children who were ill or lost that were quite similar. Hopefully the accounts I've chosen will give a full picture of the ways in which angels interact with our world.

The last two chapters of the book are slightly different from the rest, in that they include a variety of accounts that didn't seem to fit into the other chapters. Some of these are perhaps of less certain provenance—there are a few that seem to be more about spirit guides, heavenly visions, or ghosts than strictly about angels. But the people who told these stories felt that they were connected to angels in one way or another, and they do add to our body of knowledge about angels.

ALL ABOUT ANGELS

What Are Angels, and Why Do They Communicate with Us?

It seems certain, based on the quantity of accounts from across the centuries and from all over the world, that there is such a thing as an angel—a spiritual presence that is able to make itself known to people. Those who believe in or practice a religion will have their own views as to how angels relate to God. Presumably, as spiritual creatures, they are closer to him than people are, and can act as messengers and agents of divine will. In fact, the word "angel" comes from the Greek *angelos*, which may well be a translation of the Hebrew word *mal'akh*, which means "messenger." This etymology suggests a being that carries messages between the human world and other realms of existence.

Humankind is a mixture of the spiritual and the earthly. We are physical beings, earthbound in our perceptions and actions. But we have a spiritual aspect; our consciousness of our selves and our perceptions of spirituality and divinity are reflections of the spiritual side of our nature. It seems that, as spiritual beings, angels have some interest in us—perhaps even a sort of fascination with us. Perhaps they see us as we see children: simple beings who may be unable to perceive everything about the world in which they live, but who are deserving of our support and guidance by virtue of their very innocence. Perhaps angels are bound to us in ways we cannot comprehend; perhaps they are executing the will of God by tending to the flawed human race.

Whatever the truth is, it's clear that angels can sometimes communicate with us, both directly and indirectly, and they can also intervene in our lives. It seems tremendously important to comprehend whatever we can about them, even if in the end we cannot fully know who they are or why they act.

Do Angels Have Wings?

People who have had encounters with angels sometimes perceive them as winged and gracious creatures resembling humans—their traditional image. This is far from being the most common vision, however. Others simply report seeing a white light, feeling a strong presence, or meeting a strange person or even an animal that helped them or communicated with them.

Surprisingly, almost all references to angels in the Bible are to wingless beings that have taken on the form of a man. The only exceptions are the cherubim and the seraphim, which are described specifically as never leaving God's side in heaven, and one mention of a winged, female angel in the Old Testament. Non-Christian mythology has rather more mentions of winged women and children as angels; Cupid is one example, depicted with wings and a bow and arrows with which he shoots lovers. Furthermore, medieval and Renaissance paintings, and Victorian ones that derived from them, often depicted angels as having wings.

The traditional image of the winged angel may have arisen over the centuries as a literal interpretation of the idea that angels are ethereal and able to fly. It also may have been influenced by early attempts to portray heaven in physical terms as a place in the sky. Angels are thus intermediaries between "down here" and "up there." What could be more natural than to envision them as great winged beings?

It seems safe to conclude, based on firsthand accounts, that angels can choose to be visible or invisible to people, and that when they are visible, the form they take can vary widely. If the person to whom they wish to make themselves known will recognize or accept them more easily in traditional form, perhaps this influences their choice of appearance. In any case, if we are lucky enough ever to have an angelic encounter, it is only a closed mind that will fail to recognize its spiritual nature.

Do We Become Angels When We Die?

The idea that we become angels after we die is a relatively recent concept. Films such as *It's a Wonderful Life* have had a powerful effect in making popular the idea that there is continuity between the worlds of humans and angels. But Frank Capra didn't invent this idea for the character of Clarence. It has been around in one form or other from at least the second century CE, as in an early text called "The Martyrdom of Polycarp." This is undoubtedly related to the idea that people have spirits that can persist after death. This may be true, but I believe there is still a clear distinction between angels and human spirits. Certainly some of the accounts I have included in this book seem to be referring to a being that is closer to a spirit (an earthbound human soul) or a spirit guide (an ascended soul) than an angel.

Sources such as the Bible seem to indicate that angels in fact predate people, and that there is no such thing as progress from the human state to an angelic state. I wouldn't presume to be able to clear up such an enduring uncertainty. But I would say this: my personal belief is that angels are a distinct kind of being, and that even if our spirits survive in this world after our death (as opposed to surviving in an afterlife), this is a different phenomenon altogether than meetings with angels. If you feel you have communicated with angels, or that you have been in touch with loved ones after their death, you will probably have your own opinion on this. But the weight of historical ideas and religious interpretation does tend toward the idea that angels and people are separate creatures, and that the relatively recent belief that people become angels after death is a misunderstanding.

What Different Religions Tell Us About Angels

The idea of messengers from the spiritual world is present in virtually all religions, no matter how ancient. One might even consider the animal spirit guides in Native American or pagan cultures to be primitive representations of angels. The earliest known depictions of winged human-like figures come from the Sumerian culture, which flourished around the Tigris and Euphrates rivers in modern-day Iraq in about 3000 BCE. The Sumerians had a complicated polytheistic religion, but it is fascinating to discover that they believed in "messengers of the gods," angelic figures who took messages between the gods and humans, and who ran errands for the gods. The Sumerians believed that each person had a "ghost"—what we would call a "guardian angel"—that stayed with that person throughout his or her life. They dedicated altars to these beings and decorated temple walls with paintings of winged human figures. Semitic tribes conquered the Sumerians around 1900 BCE and took these beliefs further, developing the idea that angels could be ranked and subdivided into categories, an idea which persisted into later Western religions. The concept of messengers from the gods almost certainly goes back further than Sumerian culture, but this is the earliest point at which we can identify the idea clearly.

The first and second millennia before Christ gave rise to some fascinating religious developments. Spread across the Middle East and Indian subcontinent were various forms of the Mithras cult. Mithras, who was venerated in these cults, at times seems closer to the concept of a guardian angel than that of a god. He is described as a friend and a messenger as well as being a representative of the sun god on earth. Zoroastrianism, which developed out of Mithraism in the Persian Empire in approximately 500 BCE, clearly described Mithras as a being who mediated between heaven and earth. The same concept was present in early Hinduism. The *Rig Veda*, one of the earliest Hindu texts, ascribed very similar qualities to "Mitra," who appears to be the same as Mithras. It is worth mentioning in passing that Mithras as a sun god also influenced later Greek beliefs, including many of the ideas about Helios, the sun god, who was regularly depicted as having a halo. This is why the image of the halo was actually avoided in early Christian art, as being pagan in origin. But later Christian artists brought the image back, thus its more recent association with saints and angels.

Zoroastrianism's basic folk beliefs clearly fed into Islam, Judaism, and Christianity, and this is especially true of how it described angels. For the Zoroastrians, there were six archangels: the Archangels of Good Thought, Right, Dominion, Piety, Prosperity, and Immorality, along with various lower ranks of angels. All were described as being male or female and associated with particular qualities. Lower down the order were guardian angels, assigned as protectors and guides throughout each person's life. This is one of the earliest clear descriptions of guardian angels, even though it is obvious in earlier cosmologies that people had encountered angels throughout antiquity.

Judaism carried on a similar description of the existence of angels. Early Judaism went to increasing lengths to categorize and name as many angels as possible. Both the canonical and apocryphal books of the Torah and Old Testament are full of mentions of angels and demons. Later on, the Kabbalists took a particular interest in angels and demons and described them in great detail.

By the time of Jesus, people's belief in angels was already an established fact. Christian theology inherited concepts relating to angels from Judaism, as well as adding elements from Greek tradition. Angels are mentioned more than three hundred times in the Bible, described as workers and messengers of God who work in both heaven and earth. Angels who are named include Gabriel, the messenger who gave Mary the news that she was to bear the divine child, and Michael the archangel. Other angels mentioned include the two men who warned Lot of Sodom and Gomorrah's impending destruction; the multitude who announced Christ's arrival to the shepherds; and the angel who escorted John in the book of Revelations and defeated Satan. Angels comforted Jesus at the Garden of Gethsemane on the evening before his crucifixion. Abraham and Lot both met with angels; an angel wrestles with Jacob, and guides Tobit. Finally, it was an angel at the empty tomb who announced Christ's resurrection. Guardian angels are also mentioned in both the Old and New Testaments as beings that protect individuals or nations.

Over the centuries, the Christian church has continued to venerate angels and to regard demons as the source of temptation and evil. The idea that Lucifer (Satan) was a fallen angel has a particular fascination as it ascribes angelic status to the dark side of humanity and makes a connection between Lucifer and God before the Fall. Milton's *Paradise Lost* and Dante's *Divine Comedy* are just two of the great literary works that talk of the communications and meetings between mankind and the angels.

We find related concepts in other religions. The Hindu tradition has angelic beings called *devas*; Buddhists have *nats*. In Tibetan Buddhism, there are more elevated angelic beings called *dakini*. Islam, which originated about six hundred years after Christ, retained the idea of angels from Zoroastrianism, Judaism, and Christianity. It is said that God revealed the Koran to the Prophet Muhammad via the angel Gabriel. In Islamic tradition, there are four archangels—Jibrail, Mikail, Israfil, and Izrail—who can often act in Allah's stead. A class of recording angels is called the *Kiram al-Katibin*. Popular Islamic tradition says that each person has a pair of scribe angels, one on the right side who records good deeds, and one on the left who makes a note of any bad deeds. A lower order of angels is the *jinn*.

When one looks at the history of angels in religion, it's immediately apparent how consistent the descriptions of the angelic realm are across millennia and across huge expanses of the globe. From Native Americans to Asian tribes to the earliest known inhabitants of the Middle East and Europe, religions have described angels as messengers from the world of pure spirit and as agents of divine intervention, and have talked about guardian angels that take a particular interest in individual people's lives. It seems unlikely that this kind of consistency could exist simply because the religions have influenced one another in certain respects. For example, there could have been little communication between ancient Hindu and northern Russian cultures, yet there are clear similarities in the way they talk about the angelic realm.

The consistent pattern we see can only be explained by the fact that all these different religions are trying to describe and explain the experiences of real people throughout history—people who have met angels, who have been rescued or influenced by angelic interventions, and who have shared their stories with each other. Religious orthodoxy has merely incorporated the reality of folk traditions and of people's everyday lives. If anything, experiences with angels and divine beings could even be seen as the starting point of religion. In mankind's encounters with angels, we have our most immediate contact with the world of spirit, and they reveal to us that there is more to life than the physical world.

Naming the Angels

Religions such as Judaism and Christianity have made many attempts to categorize the angels, with detailed lists of the angels' names, and of the various classes of angels. It is open to discussion whether this quest can ever be successful. The angels reveal themselves to people only in a selective and unpredictable way, and no matter how hard we try to divine the truth about them, it may simply be impossible. It is nonetheless interesting to look at the ways in which people have tried to document the angelic realm.

In Christian tradition, the order of angels was formalized in the fifth century by St. Dionysius the Areopagite, in *The Celestial Hierarchy*. He ranked the types of angels as follows:

First Choir:	Second Choir:	Third Choir:
Seraphim	Dominations	Principalities
Cherubim: Virtues	Archangels: Thrones	Powers: Angels

Traditionally it has been believed that the first choir remains in heaven and contemplates the goodness of God, and the second choir regulates the running of the universe, while the third choir are those who are most closely linked to the affairs of humans. This listing clearly reflects medieval theology with its emphasis on categories and hierarchies. The fact that the third choir includes principalities, which have responsibility for nations, tribes, towns, and cities, is interesting to contemplate. If this is accurate, it implies that such political distinctions are innate parts of the ordering of the universe. It also implies that heaven's relationship to the human world is rather like that of a distant imperial capital to its provinces. This concept would have made absolute sense to those in the Middle Ages who had no other way of thinking about the world. But it does raise the question of whether this list of ranks is based more on human experience and extrapolation than it is on actual knowledge.

We can find many other details about angels in scripture and apocryphal religious texts. Here is a list of the archangels:

Enoch 1:	Enoch 3:	Christian Gnostics:
1. Uriel	1. Mikael	1. Michael
2. Raphael	2. Gabriel	2. Gabriel
3. Raguael	3. Shatqie	3. Raphael
4. Michael	4. Baradiel	4. Uriel
5. Zerachiel	5. Shachaqiel	5. Barachiel
6. Gabriel	6. Baraqiel	6. Sealtiel
7. Remiel	7. Sidriel	7. Jehudiel

Elsewhere we find the following types of angels listed:

Healing Angels
Cleric Angels
Angels of Judgment
Angel of Announcement
Angel of Death
Angel of Mercy
Angel of Music
Angel of Punishment

Fallen Angel

Half-Angel

Accusing Angel

Nephilim

Overseer

Reaper

Warrior Angel

You can also find directories of the angels, giving details of their names, their attributes, and their personal preferences, in books or on the Internet.

Perhaps this is contradictory, but my feeling is that when we see lists of these sorts, we should be simultaneously open-minded and skeptical. We should be skeptical because there was a great tendency in medieval theology and philosophy to see categorization as a substitute for thinking. Following Aristotle, many thinkers devoted great energy to the production of detailed subdivisions of all aspects of heaven and earth. Certain numbers such as seven and nine were seen as magical, especially by the Gnostics and alchemists, but also by others who should have known better, and thus many important areas were divided into numerically suitable categories: seven archangels, seven spheres, the seven seas, seven ranks of angels, nine realms of heaven and earth, and so on. This kind of list in particular seems very much a throwback to that kind of thinking.

Furthermore, the world of spirit is something that has always attracted a certain element of charlatanism. Because it is an unknowable world, there will always be those who will try to earn our reverence by claiming to know more about it than is humanly possible. This makes me suspect that some of the details that are repeated about specific angels and ranks of angels may have been invented by the unscrupulous to exploit the genuine interest that people have always felt in these beings.

But having said this, the sources we find for these categories and lists in scripture and elsewhere may also derive from genuine divine revelation. It is certainly possible that particular angels have appeared to people throughout history and that they have particular characteristics. It is beyond the scope of this book to fully examine all these possibilities. Nothing in this book proves or disproves the categorizations of angels that appear in both ancient and contemporary texts. If you wish to know more about such ways of understanding the angelic realm, there are many books that give more detail than I have space for here.

It concerns me that there are people who will charge money for contacting your guardian angel, or for identifying the angel you may have met in a particular encounter. Others claim to be able to channel messages from the angels and, again, often profit from doing this. I think it is best to be skeptical of such claims. It seems inappropriate to claim absolute knowledge of the angelic realm; clearly the angels only reveal what they wish to. But beyond this, it seems disrespectful to claim to have some kind of power over, or exclusive arrangement with, the angels. Remember this: if angels want to speak to you or help you, they are perfectly capable of doing so without any need for intervention by so-called experts.

Researching Angels

I have mentioned my belief that it is presumptuous to claim complete knowledge of the angelic realm. So what do I seek to gain by research into people's meetings with angels? What do I think it is possible for us to discover? Firstly, I think that it is important to take as broad a view of angels as possible. By viewing a large number of different accounts of encounters with angels, we can work out for ourselves what we think is the truth.

It is natural that we want to know as much as we can about angels. It is also natural that this desire may sometimes lead us into irrational or occult beliefs. Various experts tell us that there are certain types of people who will be allowed to see angels, or that there are particular signs that reveal the presence of an angel to the uninitiated. One example of this is the widely believed superstition that if you see a white feather, that is a sign that an angel is nearby. Another example is the theory that there are particular numbers or words that also tend to be associated with angels when you come across them.

The problem with such superstitions is that they take advantage of the human tendency toward irrationality. Once we hear the idea that white feathers reveal the presence of angels, we will start to notice every white feather we see, and to give it importance that far outstrips what we would previously have felt. This is not a silly thing to do; it is simply a result of the way that the human mind works. We can't take in all the information we receive, so we select what to focus on according to what is uppermost in our mind. Illusionists and hucksters have long taken advantage of this tendency in designing their tricks.

I don't mean to unfairly criticize such beliefs. They are harmless, even if they seem to me to be unlikely or far-fetched. But they are also examples of the way that the gap between our desire to know about angels and the amount of direct experience we have can lead us into strange perceptions. The best antidote to this kind of thinking is to find out as much as possible about the real experiences people have had with angels. The more we read about angels, the more we understand the reality of the angelic realm. If even a fraction of the stories I have compiled here are genuine accounts of angelic encounters, then the logical conclusion is that the angelic realm lies all around us. It is a spiritual plane that coexists with the physical plane on which we live. People do not meet angels because of their religion or beliefs. They meet them because the angels choose at that moment to make themselves known, and they do so for a reason.

Ideally I would like this book to be much longer. I could have included an enormous number of accounts, which would all cast more and more light on the world of angels. But the range and variety of accounts here does prove how common encounters with angels are, and how important the intervention of angels in human affairs can be. However, this cannot lead us to any firm conclusions about the divine world that lies beyond the angelic realm. If angels are messengers and helpers, they clearly are messengers from the divine realms that lie beyond the angelic realm, inaccessible to the human mind.

The presence of angels in our world should in itself be enough to re-energize our faith in the divinity of the universe and to remind us that the physical plane on which we dwell is only one of many planes of existence. My research is thus useful in helping us to understand as much as we can about angels, and also because it redirects our minds to the question of what lies beyond, and how we should live our lives if we are convinced that angels are a part of this world too.

Believing in Angels

One of my correspondents asked me, "Do you think it can be bad for you to believe in angels?" Personally, I can't see any possible harm that can come from it. However, some religious writers have taken the viewpoint that veneration of angels can become the equivalent of idolatry—that by focusing our faith on angels, we are neglecting to bear in mind the supremacy of God.

It is relevant at this point to explain my own religious viewpoint, as it may affect my view on this subject. I was brought up in a strict Catholic environment and spent the first part of my life following the Catholic faith. As I grew older, I came to question my beliefs, particularly why any one church should be regarded as being superior to any other. I studied other religions and found they all had a great deal in common. I am still a Christian, and I am still fascinated by the areas of agreement between the religions. For this reason, the subject of angels is of particular interest. An aspect of spirituality that is common to so many different faiths around the world seems to be highly significant.

I find angels to be a great source of inspiration about the real world of spirit that informs the faiths of the world, and therefore nothing but a positive force in one's life.

Another correspondent said that she firmly believed that it was only those who believed in angels in the first place who could hope to meet with them. She advised that if you wanted to meet with angels, you should try to believe in them as strongly as possible.

From reading historical accounts and the letters I received on the subject, it seems to me that angels can appear to pretty much anyone, regardless of their faith, religion, or moral qualities. Angels appear for many different reasons, and I can't believe that they would stop to consider whether or not a particular person believes in them strongly enough to be worth communicating with.

Furthermore, angels are not like the fairies in children's books, who only live because we believe in them. They are there whether or not we believe. However, if we don't keep an open mind, it is possible that we may meet an angel and not even realize what has happened. So in that respect there is an element of truth in what my second correspondent wrote: those who believe in angels are more likely to see them, but only because they are more likely to recognize them when they appear. On the other side of the coin, it is perhaps also true that those who believe strongly in angels may perceive them where there is only simple providence, coincidence, or sheer luck. Perhaps if you believe strongly enough, you may ascribe any piece of good fortune to angels rather than looking for earthly causes.

But is it so bad if we occasionally ascribe a happy or fortunate event to angels when it might have a more mundane explanation? When we are looking for angels, perhaps we are also more ready to celebrate the angelic side of humans, or to recognize the miraculous aspects of our everyday lives. In other words, if you believe that angels exist and intervene in the human world, that belief has real consequences for how you view your life and make moral choices. When we believe in angels, we have faith that the divine is something that is near to us every day.

ANGELS IN TIMES OF CRISIS

Angels seem most likely to appear to us when we are in a period of crisis. If an angel could stay hidden and watch while we get help from other people, they probably would do so, but if the only way they can help is by becoming visible to us, then that is what they may do.

If angels are here partly to protect and watch over people, as many believe, it is no wonder we are likely to see them or hear them when we are in trouble or anxious and frightened about something in our lives. Sometimes they simply provide us with much-needed emotional support; in other cases, they intervene directly. The more dramatic examples of angelic intervention are included in a later chapter.

MARTIN, 40
Vancouver, Canada

Our second child was born with a rare heart condition that meant that he was unlikely to live for more than a few years. A lot of his life was spent in the hospital, as he was very frail and needed regular treatments. It was terrible for my wife and I. We loved him as much as any other child, but we knew he wasn't going to make it in the end. In a situation like that, you want to inoculate yourself by not loving him so much but, if anything, you actually love him even more. We had this very intense involvement in every moment of his life. His older sister was three and found it hard to understand. Until then she had been an only child, and now everything was turned on its head. Every day we had to go to the hospital and she had a hard time. But we tried to explain it to her, and she loved her brother too.

I saw angels several times at the hospital. Once I was walking to the room where my son was, and from about twenty yards away I saw a man standing in the room, but when I got there, he was gone. Another time, I was dozing in the chair in the corner late at night, while my wife read a book to Charles. He was giggling and it woke me up. As I looked up, I saw a shining figure standing behind my wife, smiling. And once when our son was very ill, I felt hands on my shoulder and looked back to momentarily see an angel standing there, comforting me.

Charles died not long before his third birthday. We'd planned a party at the hospital, but instead we had to have a funeral. I didn't see the angels at the funeral, but

I absolutely knew that they were there. It helped me to know that.

We had another child a year after that. We called her Celeste, because both my wife and I felt that the angels had been there for us when we needed them. I think about Charles every day, but we have to go on with living our lives and doing everything we can for our daughters.

Susannah, 43
Guildford, England

My father's funeral was a strange event. Not everyone in the family was getting along, so there were tensions between my mother and my brother, and my uncle hadn't spoken to my cousin, his daughter, for some years. But there we all were.

My dad had been ill for a few years, so his death wasn't a complete surprise. Nonetheless, I was still coming to terms with the idea that I'd never be able to talk to him again. I don't actually think it had really sunk in. I'd been away when he died, and by the time I came back a few days afterward, everyone in the family had already gotten over the initial shock and had started to sort and give away his possessions. I remember they'd even set up a time to take all his books to the local charity shop. I mean, it's petty, but I wanted some of those books, and I know he would have wanted me to have them rather than just throwing them away. I kept a few things, but it was so fraught and complicated.

The funeral was on a really hot day, one of the hottest July days. We were in this little crematorium, in the nearest town, and we were all sweating and too hot. One of my dad's favorite songs was "Moon River," and my mother had chosen this as the song to be played. But the organist was terrible. I mean, that sounds unfair, but my dad was a lovely piano player, quite jazzy and laid-back, and most of us learned how to play from him. We're quite a musical family. And this organist played "Moon River" as this atrocious dirge. He was trying to be somber, I suppose, but he made a terrible hash of it. None of us knew where to look. I caught my uncle's eye at one point, and he was almost laughing, knowing what my dad would have said. Something rude, no doubt, and I nearly laughed too. But then I felt terrible.

It's like that when someone close to you has just died. Your emotions are all over the place. One minute you can feel quite normal, and the next it all comes back to you. When my mum told me my dad was dead, I couldn't cry. She wanted to fetch me hot sweet tea, and all I could think was how I didn't like tea with sugar in it, so why would I want a sweet tea now? Then, after she left, I cried my eyes out, but at the time I think she couldn't understand it. She just felt like I didn't react properly or something.

So at the funeral I was feeling terrible because there we all were and it just wasn't quite right. Even the song was wrong, and a moment after having nearly laughed, I nearly started crying. And even though that would have been a more appropriate reaction, I still didn't want to be there sobbing with everyone looking at me.

And that's when it happened. I looked up at the corner of the room and I saw this white light. It started as a small patch of light and then it started to open up wider. This light just started to flood the room and no one else seemed to see it. It was deafening, if you know what I mean. I couldn't really hear what was going on. Then there was a voice, which seemed to me to come from the light, and it just said, "It's time to say goodbye." Nothing else, just that, but it was like this voice was speaking in my head. And then suddenly the light was gone, and the room was normal. No one else reacted.

I thought, that's exactly right. I'm worrying about how I feel, and how everyone else feels, and if this is going well or not, when the only thing that matters is that I'm here to say goodbye to my dad. And that's what I did. I sat and I thought about my dad, as he was when I was a kid, playing with me. And how he was when he was older; he always so proud of me, even when I wasn't doing so well. And I wished him well and said goodbye to him in my heart. In spite of all the things that weren't quite right that day, I felt like I really had managed to say goodbye. Of course, the grieving goes on forever in some ways, but maybe it doesn't even start properly until you manage to say goodbye.

Laurence, 37
Blackburn, England

My grandfather fought in Normandy on D-Day. He didn't tell me much about it. In general, he didn't like to talk about the war. He saw some terrible things, and I think the way that they dealt with it then was just to keep it all inside. No point upsetting other people is how he'd have seen it.

But one time we were talking about religion and I was making fun of people who believe in angels. I'm more open-minded now, but when I was younger I liked to think I knew everything. He told me one small story about D-Day. He was with a group of British soldiers who got stranded away from their unit. There was total confusion everywhere. Mud, smoke, swampy ground, ditches and tangled hedges. They were hiding down in a ditch. There had been shots from a sniper that hit close by. He said it was the nearest he came to being killed in the entire war.

He said they were lying there, shaking with fear, trying to work out if it was more dangerous to stay there or run for it, and he looked up at the sky. He swore that he saw angels above them, just floating in the sky. He wouldn't describe them, just said he knew what they were. He didn't know if they were there to look after them or take them away—that was exactly what he said. He said after all, why would angels help either side in a war? All the soldiers are innocent, and angels wouldn't want anyone to die.

He wouldn't say any more about it. I guess he told me just to make me think about what I'd been saying, but still, he didn't really want to talk about the war. I've always had the idea that he saw friends die in the war, but I don't know the exact facts. I'm sorry I didn't try to make him tell me more now, but you don't think that way. I figured, if he didn't want to tell me, that was his business.

Carol, 36
Hong Kong, China

My husband walked out on me the day after my thirty-first birthday. He'd been sleeping with a friend of mine. At least, I thought she was a friend, but how can someone like that be a friend? How could she do that to me? I was absolutely distraught. I was missing work, not sleeping, not eating. Just lying in bed too miserable to move.

One night I had a dream, so maybe you could just write it off as being meaningless. But it was so vivid and so clear to me when I woke up that I believe that there was something real about it. A woman in white clothes, very beautiful, came to me. I felt like she was someone I knew. It was like meeting a long-lost friend that until then I had forgotten about somehow, but I was so pleased to see her. And she came up to me in the street; it was somewhere like the local shopping mall, with lots of people walking by, not paying any attention. She just came straight up and hugged me. I realized I'd been cold and shivering, but now there was this incredible warmth that spread from her through my entire body. She didn't feel hot—in fact, she was cool to touch—but as she pressed her cheek against mine I could feel this warmth coming into me, and soothing and relaxing me all over. It was an incredible feeling. I'll never forget it.

After that, I got myself back together, starting coping again. For a few days after that dream, I was actually quite serene. It was like I could see things from a great height and realized that this was just a moment in eternity, and that I had too many blessings in my life to be lying in bed pitying myself. Of course, nothing completely changes overnight, but something like that can really help you start getting things together. I never saw her again, but I always hope that I might meet her somewhere, or even see her in a dream again.

Tim, 28
Birmingham, England

I had a nervous breakdown when I was nineteen. It sounds silly now, but I thought aliens were trying to take over the world. I was scared of electricity, because I thought that the electricity and radio waves in the air were being hijacked by aliens to control us. I saw shapes and patterns in the air, which I thought were these waves. I saw ghostly shapes in the air and heard snatches of conversation from unseen people as I walked around the city. The voices weren't talking to me, but they were there. If anyone tried to tell me otherwise, I thought they were being controlled by aliens, so I pretended to go along with what they said and then went away and got on with my mad ideas.

I managed to move out of town, to a rundown cottage, so that I wouldn't be surrounded by so much electricity. I dropped out of college, lost a lot of friends, and ran up big debts for things I couldn't afford. I used to wear a cap that was lined with metal (an old metal bowl I found) because I thought that would deflect the radio waves. All in all, I was pretty crazy.

One day, I was out walking in the countryside; I often went for long walks. It was a pretty miserable gray day and there was no one else around. I was walking along the towpath of the canal when a man came through a gate and started walking next to me. He was just a normal-looking man, a bit older than me. He started talking to me, and he seemed very trustworthy and sensible. I immediately decided that he wasn't an alien and that I could trust him. So I started telling him all about it. After we walked past some electricity pylons, I showed him the metal lining in my hat, and then put it back on. I explained about the shapes I saw in the air.

He was quite understanding. Rather than telling me I was mad, he asked questions so that I explained more and more about what I saw, and the reasons I had started to think these things. After a while, he asked me if I had considered the possibility that the things I saw had another explanation. He said that it was possible that the voices I heard and the shapes I saw were real, but that aliens weren't the explanation. Actually, I had never considered any other reason. I told him this, but said that I knew that electricity was part of the problem, and that even if it wasn't aliens, there was definitely something there.

We walked for a while in silence, and then he asked if he could show me something. I said yes. So he waved his hand in front of us, and suddenly everything I could see changed. The gray weather disappeared completely and there was bright sunshine. For the first time, I could clearly see the waves and shapes of power billowing around the electricity pylons and telephone poles on the road by the canal. There were waves flowing from one to another. But also I saw people everywhere. There were people walking past, oblivious to us, some happy, some sad, in all kinds of clothes. And there were angels walking around, dressed in white—clearly angels, because of the light that surrounded them. I looked at my companion and saw that he was an angel too. He waved his hand again and it all disappeared and went back to normal. We walked in silence for a while.

"What was that?" I finally asked. He told me that he had given me a glimpse of the world the way he saw it. I asked who the people were, but he told me that it didn't matter. He said that maybe I had been seeing tiny bits of what he saw, and that I had believed I was seeing aliens when in fact I was seeing something quite different. This made a lot of sense to me. We kept walking for a while, then he walked off in a different direction. He told me to think about what he had shown me.

I went home and went to bed. I slept a long time, about thirty hours, then woke up extremely hungry. I walked outside and looked around for the waves and voices. I couldn't see or hear them, but I realized that I was looking for something completely different now. I wasn't looking for the malevolent powers I had seen previously. Now I saw the electricity and radio waves and something that was simply there, flowing around in the atmosphere. I saw the voices as being faint echoes of angels or ghosts or whatever.

I've always been reluctant to talk about this, because it was how I recovered from my nervous breakdown, but the one or two people I've talked to about it have reacted as though this was just as crazy as seeing aliens. But I think that it really was an angel who realized that I was lost in confusion, and who helped me out by giving me a hint that I was on the wrong track. The idea that we are surrounded by angels is not a frightening one; it is quite a reassuring one. And once I came to terms with that, I started to see how strangely I had been behaving. I went back to college, in a different place, and managed to get my life back together. I heard the voices a few more times, but after that I wasn't scared or alarmed when it happened.

AIDAN, 48
Dublin, Ireland

My father died a while ago and, although it was terribly sad for both myself and my two sisters, it wasn't entirely unexpected. He was seventy-eight, for a start, and he hadn't been himself since my mother had died a couple of months before. It wasn't that he was particularly ill or anything; it was just that he'd had enough and he didn't really want to go on without her.

He lived just outside Dublin and I'd managed to get to see him quite a lot over those months, but whenever I tried to get him to do stuff or just perk up a bit, he'd say that he wasn't really interested, except for maybe having a couple of pints at lunchtime. He wasn't depressed or bitter; he just reckoned he'd had a good life and all he wanted to do was to wait it out until he could see my mother again. He said that I wasn't to worry and that I wasn't to feel too sad when he went, because the angels would look after him like they were already looking after her.

My sisters tried talking to him as well, but they were missing our mother too and I think they understood better than I did. The only thing my father was insistent on was that we were to have a good time at his funeral— drink a toast to him, he said, and then have a party. He'd love to be there to see it, he said.

After he died and we were going through his things, one of my sisters found a padded envelope under the bed addressed to me. We all sat round while I opened it. Inside there was a note in his slightly shaky handwriting that said, "Remember what I said, Aidan, and have a drink on me. Put this behind the bar at the Queen's Head." Along with the note was a sheaf of bank notes that added up to just over five hundred pounds. (This was before we got stuck with the Euro, of course.) It was typical of my father to pay for his own wake and to leave instructions on how to go about it. We decided that if that was what he wanted, then that was what we'd do.

The funeral was fine, and then we all went to the pub. I made a very short speech thanking everybody for coming and telling them that the drinks were on my dad, who had obviously known what he was doing. There was a lot of laughter, and then everyone got started on some serious drinking. It was a great atmosphere but, after an hour or so, I just wanted to be on my own, so I went into the bar next to the room where we were having the party. I just stood and looked out of the window at the field opposite. To tell you the truth, I was suddenly feeling very emotional and I didn't want to cry in front of all the guests.

It was odd, because I'd been fine dealing with all the arrangements for the funeral and the wake, but now that it was all sorted out, it came home to me that I'd lost both of my parents within about two months and that I'd never be able to see them again. The door opened and my sisters came in—they must have seen me leave and guessed how I was feeling—and they stood on either side of me and each took one of my arms and looked out of the window with me.

After a minute or so, my sister Eileen said, "Look at those people in the field. What are they doing there?" There were four people standing in the field opposite, looking at the pub, as far as I could tell. I thought that the sun must be going down, because all of their faces were glowing with a pink and orange light that rippled over their features. They must have noticed us looking at them, because they all smiled at once, like they'd been caught out doing something they weren't supposed to do. The light from their faces seemed to wash across the field into the room where we were standing. I couldn't make out the faces of the two people on either end of the line of four, but I could sense that all they knew was peace and happiness, and that they were sending those feelings to the couple between them and into my sisters and me.

Then my sisters gripped my arms tighter and we all realized together that the couple in the center was our mother and father. We'd put photographs of them on all the bars in the Queen's Head and I thought for a moment that we were just seeing a reflection of the picture in the window, but I knew in my heart that it wasn't that at all. My father had been right. The angels were looking after him and my mother, just as he had said and, somehow, he'd managed to convince them to let him have a look at the party that he had paid for and wanted to be at. My sisters and I stood and looked at our parents and their guardian angels until the light faded and we realized that they'd gone.

I still miss my father and mother, but I know that they're happier than they ever were and that they are always looked after. I'll always be grateful that the angels that care for them came to let us know.

LISA, 46
California, USA

There was a period in my life when I became extremely depressed. I was taking sleeping pills because I hadn't been able to sleep due to anxiety attacks. I spent the days in a fog of misery and uncertainty. It's impossible to imagine how crippling depression can be unless you have suffered from it. It gets to the stage where nothing can make you happy. You see sunshine and it seems harsh and unpleasant. Even birds singing sounds threatening or harsh. There's nothing nice in the world, at least in the way you perceive it.

I kept having a vision of a man's face. I thought it was trying to threaten me. It would come into my head, but I would push the vision away. I would sit and concentrate on thinking about nothing in order to avoid letting this face affect me. But all the time it was getting stronger and stronger. There was a light around the man's hair and he looked very serious. I don't know why he scared me so much, but for the longest time, weeks or months, I wouldn't let him in.

I was getting more and more exhausted and weak from depression and from not looking after myself properly. Finally one night I was too tired and I decided that, whoever it was, I couldn't resist any longer. It was in the middle of the night, and I remember making a conscious decision to allow myself to see the face clearly rather than shying away.

Then there was a man in the room with me. It's hard to explain, because I know he wasn't really there, but at the time it seemed real. He asked, "Why have you been trying to keep me away? I only want to help." I told him I was scared, and he said he understood. Then he sat and held my hand and talked to me about all the things I was depressed about. It was a long conversation. I won't tell you all that had happened to me, but trust me, I had been through some dark times. I realized very quickly that he knew everything about me and there was no point trying to pretend. He was some kind of angel, and he knew exactly what I had been going through.

But also he knew that for me everything was a matter of free will. I remember he said many times, "I can't force you to be happy. What you think and feel is your decision. You can't always help what happens to you, but you can decide how to react to it." And at the same time, he was also telling me that a lot of how I felt wasn't necessary. I could have been reacting differently.

After we had finished speaking, he left me and I went to sleep. I spent the next few days thinking about everything he had said. I couldn't shake off the depression just like that, but I realized that there were choices I could make. I could force myself to leave the house, even though the thought of doing it scared me. I could decide to see the sunshine and feel its warmth and take pleasure in that. I could enjoy little things and try to work my way up toward greater happiness.

It was also a great consolation knowing that the angel cared for me and had chosen to come and try to help me. It's not that it made me feel special in any way; in fact, he went out of his way to tell me that it wasn't just me, that there were other people he tried to help. But he also told me that if I ever really needed him, he would be there again. In itself that helped, because rather than seeing everything as a downward spiral, I was able to see that there are options, and even in the most extreme times there is someone who would know and care. I am not alone in the world.

DANA, 46
Texas, USA

Last year I was on a flight back from Australia when there was a problem with the engines. It was a bad flight in any case, a night flight where there was turbulence, and the plane was swinging from side to side in an alarming manner. We had to keep our seatbelts on for hours.

Then, still about an hour out to sea, there was an audible bang outside. I was in a window seat and, even though it was dark, I thought I saw a flash of something near the wings. The captain eventually announced that there was a problem with the engines and that he had had to turn one of them off for safety. He assured us that the plane was perfectly safe on the remaining engines, but of course people were pretty scared. He said that he would need to land early and that he was asking for clearance from Los Angeles.

Everyone was very quiet for a while, and a few people were praying out loud. I wished they wouldn't, as it seemed to make it more frightening for others, even though I understand it was a comfort to them. Because we still had turbulence, every little bump and drop was terrifying. Each time, my whole stomach lurched as though this was it and we were going to dive. But each time it was just a little bit of turbulence. The crew took us through all the safety stuff again, and this time it seemed very real when they started explaining about lifejackets and whistles.

The captain announced that we had been cleared to land and would be there in about thirty minutes. At this point, I looked out of the window and I saw the angels. They were white and very clear. They were hovering over the wings, if that makes sense. I mean, we were going how fast? Flying speed, which is very fast. So they must have been going fast too, to keep up, but they didn't seem to be making any effort. There were three of them that I could see, and they were just there over the wing. I looked around to see if anyone else could see, but no one seemed to be looking. And then when I looked back I wasn't so sure I could see them. We started going in and out of clouds and I just caught one more glimpse of them.

The landing wasn't great. With the engine out, I guess the pilot had some problems, so we bounced a bit and a few people bumped their heads slightly. But really, it was the fear that was bad, not the impact. There were fire crews and medical teams all waiting on the tarmac, which again made it seem very vivid that we had been at risk.

Knowing the angels were there, I don't know what to say. Maybe they saved us. Maybe they were there because we were close to death. Or maybe they were just there to keep an eye on us and help if we needed it. I was still scared, but knowing they were there made me much less scared than I would otherwise have been.

TIMOTHY, 77
Colorado, USA

I had a bad fall once when I was rock climbing. It must be forty years ago now, would you believe? I was with my climbing partners and we were going up a fairly tricky section. It was actually a stupid accident because it was completely needless. We were tied together and doing everything very carefully. Then we stopped for some food and water on a ledge. There was plenty of room, and we took off all the safety stuff while we ate.

Afterward, before we put the gear back on, I walked a little way along the ledge, and I just went too near the edge. A whole section crumbled under my foot, and I ended up sliding down a slope and over the edge. There was nothing anyone could do to stop me, but I was being careless in the first place, so it was completely my own fault.

The fall was something like a hundred feet—quite a long way, really. As I fell, I didn't have my life flashing before my eyes, like you're supposed to. Instead, I saw very clearly two angels falling with me, and twisting in the air alongside me as I flailed my arms around, trying to get into a better position. They weren't like real people, but shining, semi-transparent figures that fell alongside me.

Then I hit and lost sight of them. I was extremely lucky because I hit on a curved bit of rock face with no jagged edges, then half-rolled, half-fell through a bush that slowed me down slightly before I fell a bit farther and hit the ground.

I broke my leg quite badly, and had scratches and bruises from the impact, but I survived. By the time my colleagues got down there, I was in some pain but I was conscious, and was even able to joke with them about how dumb I had been. They managed to get me down far enough for help to come and I was fine in the end. My leg always had a slightly funny twist from the way the bone set, but I'm still going strong.

I don't know if I saw the angels because I was close to death. Sometimes I wonder if they saved me. They seemed to be swirling around me, and maybe they either slowed me down or helped me to land in the slightly lucky spot I hit, where I was slowed down before the final impact. Either way, I definitely saw them, and no one can tell me anything different.

Debbie
Wyoming, USA

A few years ago, I was having a really hard time. It was one of those times in my life when I felt that everything was going wrong for me. My life was a mess. One day my washing machine broke down and then my car was stolen overnight. Both things happened within twenty-four hours. I had become so depressed that I seriously considered ending it all.

Without my car, I had to walk to the store to buy milk and cat food. The store was quite far away and most of the walk was uphill, so I was not looking forward to it. It was one of those times when you feel utter despair. I made it to the store and, as I was walking away with my milk and my cat food, a woman offered me a ride in her car.

I was so grateful I made a silent little prayer of thanks to God. As we drove away, the woman began talking about prayers and God. I thought this was funny, given my recent little prayer. The woman told me that God would answer my prayers because I had not wavered in my faith, despite my current hard times. She said that everything would work out.

Just after I got home, my brother-in-law called to ask if I had any need for a different car, as he and my sister were buying a new one. About a week after that, I got a good job in a local government office and things really began to look up. The more I think about it, I'm sure that the woman was an angel, sent to pick me up in my hour of need.

KIM
Winnipeg, Canada

I had a bad break-up with a boyfriend while I was in college. I was so upset that I had even decided to give up on my studies so that I wouldn't have to see him around campus. There was one particular day when I was in the dining hall, crying into my coffee, when a girl came up and asked if she could sit with me.

She talked to me for a long time and I really did begin to feel better. I decided then and there that I would finish my course, graduate, and get a good job. I felt so much stronger for having talked it through with this girl.

I asked for her name and room number so I could keep in touch. She said she was called Kate and her room number was sixty-five.

When I went to look for her, there were only room numbers up to sixty, and when I checked with the registration office, her name was not on the current list of students. I think she was sent to guide me to make the right decision for my future, despite my feelings at the time. I'm glad she did.

EVERYDAY ANGELS

It was fascinating to discover how many people encounter angels on a daily basis. Perhaps these are people who are so open to the spiritual world that they can easily perceive the angels around us. Or perhaps, having once met an angel, it becomes easier to detect the signs and clues that are an indication of an angelic presence. This might mean that people who have had a more dramatic encounter with an angel, such as an intervention in a crisis or a near-death experience, then go on to have everyday meetings with angels.

Unlike the accounts in the previous chapter, in the following stories the presence of angel is not something that happens in times of great stress or emotion. Rather, it's a simple yet profound reassurance that we are not alone in this world.

PETER, 32
Dublin, Ireland

My mother was an extraordinary woman. She raised six of us by herself, and it can't have been easy as we were little terrors. But she was always laughing and happy, and even though she never had a minute to rest, it never seemed to wear her down.

She used to tell me stories about angels and how they looked after us. I even saw angels a few times. My mother would be washing the dishes, and the angel would be sitting at the kitchen table watching her, but then if I blinked and looked again she would be gone. She was a woman about my mother's age, tall, with a nice face. Sometimes I would come down in the night for a glass of water when I couldn't sleep, and there would often be two angels sitting in the front room. They didn't look up when I came through, but again, they would disappear if I tried to look straight at them.

Whenever I think of my mother, I think of the chaos of that house, of children everywhere running around shouting, of my mother laughing and carrying piles of clothes, and of the angels sitting calmly, watching everything.

SARAH
Georgia, USA

I'm convinced I saw an angel once. It was at Christmas and I would have been about seven years old. I always loved our Christmas tree. We could never afford a real one, but we had a silver artificial one covered with an assortment of really gaudy baubles that had been in the family for years.

One night I crept downstairs just to look at the tree, and as I turned to look at it, I saw an angel standing next to it, facing it. The angel had huge wings and was nearly as tall as the tree. I still remember that moment, although I have no idea what it meant. I wasn't frightened, more awestruck really. It was as if I was given confirmation that Christmas that angels really do exist. That experience and knowledge has stayed with me all my life.

GINA, 36
Melbourne, Australia

When I'm cleaning the house, or out shopping, or doing some silly household thing, I often think about my three children at school. I've always had a slightly panicky feeling about them being away from me, ever since the first day I had to say goodbye to them at the school gates. I worry about what they are doing and if they are safe. Then I see this figure in my mind, a woman who smiles at me and shakes her head, like she's saying, "What are you worrying about? Come on, Gina, they're fine." I've always thought that, even though I worry, there is a guardian angel watching over them.

HELENA, 25
Birmingham, England

I've always seen angels, since I was a child. I used to see my guardian angel in the night, standing in the corner of my room or at the bottom of the bed, looking at me. She is tall with a kind face. She doesn't have wings or anything like that. She's just a normal-looking woman, but with a very wise expression. When I was very small it used to scare me, and I'd shout for my parents, but as I got older I got used to it. I mentioned it to my parents once or twice and they either laughed or looked a bit concerned about it, as though I was mad, so I realized it was something you didn't really talk about.

In my teens I read everything I could about angels, and I realized that lots of people see their guardian angels, but not everyone. I'm not sure why. Maybe it depends on whether or not you want to see them. I haven't been in any life-threatening situations, so it's hard to say if my angel has ever helped me. Who knows what might have happened?

I've seen other angels a few times. At school I used to see them standing behind children or walking along the corridor. And I used to see my mother's when she was ill, although I couldn't see its face. It was a white glow in the room, rather than a visible person.

I don't believe that you can talk to angels unless they really need to, but I smile at mine when I see her and she smiles back. So I know she is there if I need her.

RACHEL
Adelaide, Australia

I saw angels in my bedroom when I was five years old. They were standing above my bed looking down on me with these beautiful faces and really kind smiles. They had the most loving, peaceful faces that I have ever seen. The whole room felt bathed in glowing white light, and I will never forget how happy I felt at that moment. My mum had just remarried, and so it was the start of a new period in all of our lives. Suddenly I felt okay about everything. I knew we were all going to be very happy. I've never seen angels since, but I do know that they are there looking out for me, and that's a nice feeling.

KELVIN, 38
Auckland, New Zealand

We are always in the company of angels. I knew this from an early age, but it is only as I've gotten older that I have learned how to see them. I prayed for a long time to meet angels, and I have always spoken to my guardian angel in my head, although he doesn't speak back. I know that someone has been looking after me, and when I've been in dangerous situations in life, it has always worked out fine. Last year I had a terrible bout of food poisoning, which made me sick for several days, but always there was a voice at the back of my mind telling me that I would be all right, and that's how it turned out.

After that I read more about angels, and started to look for them around me as I walk around, and I've discovered that they are visible sometimes. You can be walking along and catch sight of one out of the corner of your eye, but if you look more closely it will be gone. They are often in white or pale clothes, and they walk the city streets the same as us. But they don't necessarily want you to see them.

Beyond that, you can actually see their outlines in the air occasionally. If you stand outside in a busy place, like in the center of town, and stay very still, looking around you intently, you can start to see outlines in the air. It's as though there is a transparent liquid or jelly shape in the air, but the light distorts slightly through it so you can catch the outlines and shapes. Often they will be walking next to people, especially young children, so it is good to look into the spaces near people, and try to look so that you can see sky behind them, because the light of the sky makes them easier to spot.

I told my friend about this, and he tried it and found that he could see them too. However, he found it rather alarming, as it made him feel that there are forces at work that are beyond his comprehension. On the contrary, I feel reassured to know that they are there. It feels as though they don't need to be seen, but aren't so concerned as to completely disguise themselves. Why should they hide from those who have faith in them? They are here to help and protect us, and so many people have seen them already.

Mona, 18
Perth, Australia

When I was a child I used to go and hide in the cupboard under the stairs sometimes. This is when I was about eight or nine. I would go there when I was feeling a bit down— nothing terrible, just little moments when I wanted to be on my own. I'd go right to the back and sit in the dark.

My parents never worked out that that was where I went. It was a big old house and it was easy to disappear. Sometimes I would be able to hear them walking around calling for me, and I'd stay quiet, then come out later when they weren't there to see.

I used to speak to my angel when I was in there. I could hear her voice very clearly. I'd tell her what I'd been doing, and about the little things that had upset me. And she'd tell me what she thought. She didn't really give me advice. She just listened and asked questions in a very kind and understanding way. I'd end up realizing for myself when I was in the wrong about something, or how I could make up with someone I'd fallen out with.

The strange thing is that I thought nothing of it at the time. I'd grown up believing in God and the angels, and it seemed perfectly normal that when I had a problem, my angel would speak to me. I had a clear image of her face, as though I had seen her when I was younger, but now I only heard her in the cupboard.

We moved house eventually and there was nowhere like that where I could go and sit in the dark. So I didn't talk to my angel for a while. And then when I tried to talk to her, I couldn't hear her voice anymore. It just drifted away like that. I think it was something to do with age. At a certain age it was very easy for me to talk to her. Later on, it became more conscious and difficult, and then it didn't come so easily. I didn't stop believing in angels. I just realized that they are there, but you can't always see them or talk to them.

KATE
Leicester, England

When I was at primary school, I used to love going for walks on my own if I was upset about anything. There was this lovely route that took me past fields of cows and buttercups, and walking by them always made me feel so much better. There's a place along the walk that we used to call Bluebell Wood, though it's really just a copse of trees with lovely flowers underneath.

One day after I had had a particularly miserable day involving sports, and also Mrs. Schofield, the French teacher, I decided to go along to Bluebell Wood on my own. As I got near, there seemed to be this lovely light coming out from the trees. It looked really beautiful.

When I was under the trees, I looked up and saw three huge angels floating above. They were huge, with great wings, and had this sort of unearthly glow about them. As I looked at them, I could feel all the stresses of the day leave me and I felt so happy and calm. It was a feeling of being able to cope with anything, really. Things seemed to work better for me at school after that, and I gradually became less of a worrier.

SARAH
Connecticut, USA

I saw an angel on a beach once. It's sort of a strange place to see one, I know, but I did. It was a summer evening and we were just sitting watching the sunset when I suddenly heard something behind me. Thinking it must be a raccoon or something, I got up to look in the trees behind us. I always loved looking for animals.

Anyway, I went a little way into the woods on my own and suddenly felt such a sense of peace. It was as if the woods were glowing with magical light. I looked up and there in front of me was an angel. She smiled at me. I'm sure this angel was female; she had such a pretty face and long golden hair.

I have always felt very special to have been blessed by an angel. Whenever I go through difficult times, I always think of that moment the angel smiled at me to give me strength and courage.

LEONARD
York, England

When my older brother and I were little, we used to play in the local graveyard. We would hide behind the tombstones or in bushes and make scary noises to whoever happened to be passing. Our favorite prank was to scare groups of girls or little old ladies—soft targets, really. The girls would always giggle when they spotted us, but I think, looking back now, that we really did scare some of the old ladies. Maybe they thought we would rob them or something.

Anyway, one cold winter afternoon we hid behind the gravestones as usual when we saw an old lady walking toward us. When she was fairly near, we leapt out from our hiding place shouting "Ooooooooooooooh!" like we were ghosts or something. But when we jumped out, the old lady seemed to have vanished.

We heard a noise behind us and when we turned around we saw this glowing gold angel-type thing. We were terrified and ran across the path and into the next section of the graveyard. When we looked back, only the old lady was there, putting some flowers by one of the headstones. She turned and looked at us, giving us this weird smile like she knew that we'd been frightened and it served us right. We never went to play in that graveyard again. I don't know what it was we saw, or even if we really saw it or just frightened ourselves, but it worked because we never went back.

Helena, 25
Naples, Italy

I believe in angels. I've never actually seen one, but I have felt their presence. There's often a lovely smell when they're around and you just know that a lovely caring being surrounds you. There are times when I ask their advice about things. I just sit down, close my eyes, and concentrate on summoning my angels to help me. After a while I feel this comforting presence. It's like someone who really loves you putting their arms around you and giving you a hug.

I always think of ways I can solve my problems at those moments. I think it's the angels helping me out, pointing me in the right direction, so to speak. It makes the world seem a much nicer place, knowing that we have angels to protect and guide us.

HEALING ANGELS

It seems clear that angels have the power to heal people. Why do they sometimes help us in illness and suffering and sometimes not? It is impossible to say. The angels know things about our spiritual life that we cannot, and it is beyond our understanding why they intervene in one case and not in another. But judging by the cases included here, it is clear that they do sometimes respond in situations where they can make a big difference, and they sometimes seem to respond to prayers or requests for help. In most of the encounters in this chapter, the angels physically healed those who were ill or injured. In a few cases, the angels seemed to be present to ease an individual's passing.

Many of those who have been helped by angels in a time of suffering have their faith and attitude toward life transformed as a result. Others have a one-time encounter that lets them know that angels are there when we need them. As ever, it seems that children are close to angels' hearts. No one likes to see a child ill or suffering, and angels seem especially likely to help out when children are afflicted. But the stories here concern people of all ages, from very young to very old. No one is beyond the love of the angels, and these stories are very clear demonstrations of this fact.

KATHY, 58
Texas, USA

I'm a nurse, and working in a hospital, you hear a lot of stories about angels. It's hard to know if that's because a hospital is a place where people are ill and in need of help, or if it is just kind of traditional, like urban legends. But once I was in a group of about fifteen nurses talking about it, and seven of them thought they had seen an angel at some point in the hospital. That's nearly half the people there.

The only time it happened to me was a long time ago now, in the seventies. There was a woman who had had a difficult birth, so she was on regular observation. The baby was fine, but he was in an incubator, so she was alone in the room. There was no husband; I can't remember if he was away, or perhaps she was on her own.

I went for the last check, close to the end of my shift at about midnight. As soon as I got there, I knew something was wrong. She was lying still and there was a lot of blood; it seemed like she was hemorrhaging. I was really scared. She was unconscious and all the indications were bad. It seemed like she might die. I just shouted for help—not very professional—and then I remembered to press the button for help. Right away a man came into the room, not a doctor or nurse, just a young man wearing normal clothes.

I asked who he was, and he said it was okay, he knew what to do. He told me to run and get help. Then he just walked over and put his palm on her forehead, very calmly. That's all. I don't know why I trusted him; he could have been anyone. But he seemed so calm and knowing. I left him there with his hand on her forehead and ran down the corridor. I was only gone about two minutes, because I ran into the doctor who was coming to deal with the emergency as he came out from the stairs.

When we got back, the man was gone. The woman was sitting up in bed, pale but awake. There was a lot of blood on the sheets, but when the doctor examined her, the bleeding seemed to have stopped of its own accord. I kept an eye on her over the next few days, and she was fine and happy. It was hard to believe how near to death she'd been. She had a beautiful child, a very delicate dark-haired baby, tiny because he had been born early, but with a lovely face. I actually remember the baby's face clearly, though I can't remember the mother's face so well. I never saw the man again.

DONALD, 41
Edinburgh, Scotland

My son David had German measles when he was little. It's usually not too serious, but he developed some kind of infection and became seriously dehydrated. The doctor came to the house three times. David was vomiting every time he ate or drank. He was thirsty all the time but finding it hard to hold down even water. He had a terrible fever; he was burning to touch. He became quite strange—his eyes were very dilated, and he was seeing things. It quite scared me because he was looking at things behind me and saying odd things about the faces he could see.

The doctor told us to stay with him and to keep giving him a drink every hour or so, even if we had to wake him up to do it, because the dehydration was the dangerous thing. He said that if things didn't improve overnight, we might have to take him to the hospital. I stayed up through the night because my wife was absolutely shattered. She didn't want to go to bed, but I told her she had to sleep for a few hours at least. When she finally gave in, she lay down and was sleeping like a log within a few moments.

I kept waking David up and getting him to drink a little. He would mutter and grumble and then fall straight back to sleep. But all the time he was asleep, he was tossing and turning. I was reading a book to try and stay awake. I'd promised my wife that if I started falling asleep I'd get her up, but I wanted her to sleep, so I tried to keep going. And then I suppose maybe I did fall asleep.

When I woke up, there was a woman standing by the bed, holding David's hand. I was terrified; I had no idea what was happening. I tried to sit up or say something but I couldn't move. I was completely paralyzed. She glanced at me and it was clear she knew I was awake, but she just looked back at David. I sat there staring at her for about five minutes, with my heart thumping, then I closed my eyes and she was gone and I could move. I jumped up and ran to David. I woke him up and gave him another drink. He drank much more than he had any of the other times, almost half a glass. He was still very hot, but this time when he lay down, he lay still and seemed to fall into a deep sleep rather than tossing and turning.

I managed to stay awake until about eight in the morning, then got my wife up and lay down for a few hours sleep myself. I didn't say anything to her about what I'd seen. I thought she'd think I was mad. I woke up at about midday and hurried in to see how David was. The fever had gone and he could sit up and drink. He'd stopped being sick, and by the evening he could even eat. He got better from there on.

ALISON, 47
Fife, Scotland

Not long after my parents died, I developed a skin condition. It gradually spread over my legs, arms, and chest— an itchy, flaking rash. It was very unpleasant. I was living in the house alone and it made coping with all the little everyday stuff very difficult. I had to try not to scratch, as it only made it worse, but nothing stopped the itching.

The doctor wasn't too clear on why it had developed. First he called it contact dermatitis and tried to narrow down the possible causes. I wore cotton clothes and bought cotton sheets. I cut down on soap and various foodstuffs and so on, but nothing helped. He decided it was either an allergy to dust, which is very hard to cope with, or psoriasis. Either way, he didn't think there was much he could do to reverse it, and he gave me an allergy cream and emollient oils to spread on it. I would have a bath and wash in this oil because soap seemed to be one of the things that made me worse. My sheets would get in a terrible state as I lay there all oily and wriggling around trying to get comfortable and get a bit of sleep.

I was in a pretty miserable state by the time it had been going on a few months. Then I had a dream where an angel came to see me. She was a tall woman, with a very pure, honest face, and I knew she was an angel immediately. She talked to me about my parents first of all, then we talked about my skin. She told me that the problem came from within me. She told me to think happy thoughts of my parents, so I remembered a day when I was about eighteen and we went to the seaside. Then she peeled away all the itching skin, as though it was just stuck onto my skin. It was very painful, like peeling a scab, but at the same time I knew she was peeling away all of the bad skin. Afterward I was left there standing with new clear skin. She told me I needed to keep thinking the happy thoughts.

When I woke up, I thought about what the angel had said and done. I haven't really explained about my parents, but I had to look after them for about ten years when they were old. My dad had Alzheimer's, and my mum was too frail to cope with him. I realized how bitter I had become about this period of my life. They had seemed to turn into quite different people when they were old. They were both very dependent where they had always been fiercely independent before. My dad used to get very angry because he couldn't accept the deterioration in his mind, and he hated forgetting stuff. It wasn't all bad, but it was very hard for me, and it was exacerbated by the fact that my two elder brothers mostly just left me to it.

Now I tried to put into practice what the angel had told me. I tried to think about the good times with my parents. I remembered some good things from the last few years, and also I remembered how they had looked after me when I was young. I also thought about particular happy days: birthdays when I was little, or the day they came to see me graduate from college and took me out for a meal.

The more I thought about this, the more I started to put the last few bad years into perspective, and the more I felt a weight lifting from my mind. I had allowed it all to get on top of me, and had got into a bad mental state without realizing that I could get away from that. The angel was absolutely right that this was the cause of my skin problem. After that, it started slowly to improve. Of course, it didn't clear up overnight like it had in the dream, but it did get much better, and within a couple of months it was mostly gone. I still had to be a bit careful about letting certain things come into contact with my skin, and I still use the emollient cream sometimes, but the worst of it was over.

I suppose a good psychiatrist might have been able to uncover the cause, but I'm not sure that the doctor ever would have been able to put me on the path to recovery. The worse my skin got, the more my mental state was deteriorating in response—it was a vicious circle in that respect. It needed an intervention from somewhere completely different to show me the way toward recovery.

CYNTHIA
Louisiana, USA

I remember that we frequently went to church in the evenings when I was a little girl. I remember this one particular evening when there was a young woman in front of us. Apparently she had been blinded in an accident when she was a teenager. She would have been about twenty, as I remember her. The doctors had said that she would never see again.

As we all joined in the service, I looked over at this young woman and she was bathed in this weird glowing light. As I looked, the outline of an angel with huge wings appeared to be enveloping her. To be honest, I felt a bit frightened and began to cry. I would only have been about twelve at the time. My mom asked me what was wrong and I told her quietly that I had seen an angel standing above the blind woman. My mom hugged me and went over to the woman. "You have been chosen for healing," I remember Mom telling her. She told her that the next time she came to church, she would be able to see.

Two weeks later I saw the woman walking up to the church without her white stick. I ran over to her to say hello, but of course she'd never actually seen me before, so she didn't know who I was. When I told her that it was me who saw the angel, she cried and hugged me and my mom and was so thankful. I've always believed in the healing powers of angels ever since.

KATHLEEN, 28
Manchester, England

My first child, a beautiful little girl, was born very prematurely and had to spend the first few weeks of her life in an incubator in the hospital's special care baby unit. I didn't get to see her until a couple of days after she was born, because I wasn't very strong either, but when I did I just stood next to the incubator and cried. She looked so tiny and perfect, but I knew that she didn't stand much of a chance after being born at twenty-two weeks. I thought it was terribly unfair.

She was lying very still and there were intravenous drips in her arms. To keep her warm, she was lying on a little knitted blanket that looked only as big as a handkerchief. One of the nurses told me that it had been made by a midwife who used to work in the unit. I thought it was wonderful that someone would do something like that in the middle of all that technology. My little girl had something to lie on that had been made with love.

For the first few days that I was able to, I sat by the incubator for as long as I could. I was only sixteen, and the father didn't want to be involved, so my mum and dad used to come in and sit with me whenever they could. Mostly, though, it was just me and my baby, who didn't even have a name yet.

The nurses were absolutely lovely, but they never went so far as to say that it would all be all right, and I was very aware of how concerned they were. There were always several of them in the ward and they checked on my baby every fifteen minutes or so to make sure that she was breathing okay and that her drips were doing whatever it was that they were supposed to.

On the third day that I spent sitting by the crib, a new nurse came to change the drips and, after she'd finished, she sat with me for a while, which was something that hadn't happened before. Her name was Anna and after she'd introduced herself she didn't say much else; she just sat and looked at my baby with me. Just before she left to get on with her other work, she put her hand on the side of the incubator near the baby's head.

My little girl opened her eyes and turned her head toward Anna's hand. It was the first time I'd seen her with her eyes open and the first time I'd seen her move and I could hardly believe it. Anna smiled and rubbed my shoulder—I didn't think anything of it at the time, but it occurred to me later that none of the other nurses had ever done anything like that, either—and then she went off to the other end of the ward and disappeared into the nurses' station.

For a week after that, every afternoon, Anna came and sat with me. She always put her hand onto the incubator and my baby always turned her head and opened her eyes to look, first at me, and then at Anna. It seemed to me that it made her happy.

Ten days after she was born, when I arrived at the incubator, my baby was strapped down to the tiny cot with little fabric ties. I nearly went mad at the duty nurse, but I shut up when she told me that it was because that tiny little mite had been dragging herself around the incubator and pulling out her drips. They'd had to have special restraints made to keep her still, because they didn't have anything small enough.

When the duty nurse was walking away, I could hear her laugh as she told one of the other nurses that I was going to be in for a lot of trouble from that one in the future. Anna showed up a few minutes later and smiled when she saw my little girl tied down to the bed. She put her hand on the side of the incubator and the baby stretched her tiny fingers out toward it. "I think she's going to be fine," Anna said, and then she wandered off to the nurses' station again.

The next day she didn't show up and I asked one of the other nurses if it was her day off. She said that there wasn't anybody called Anna working in the unit, but that it was understandable that I might make a mistake because of all the stress I'd been under.

I went back to the incubator and realized that we had been visited by an angel who had helped my baby come back to life. She never visited again—at least not when I could see her, but I think that she sometimes was there because, every so often, my baby would open her eyes wide and stretch out her hand as if someone had their hand close to her head.

We left the hospital after about six weeks. My daughter is now twelve years old, has the constitution of an ox, and is named after the angel who helped to save her life.

MARIA, 35
Lisbon, Portugal

I am a singer, and a few years ago I had a real problem with my voice. I was losing my voice very badly, and it hurt to sing full voice. I tried resting it for a few weeks and going back, but it was just as bad after a day or two. The doctors diagnosed nodules on my throat. They said it was unlikely to improve without an operation. This would have been terrible for me, as it would have been a major disruption in my work, with no guarantee that my voice would ever be back to normal.

Coming from the doctors, I felt desolate. I was walking down a hill, feeling very sad and not knowing what to do. A young man coming the other way stopped me. He asked me how I was, because I looked so sad. He was about twenty, with very piercing eyes. I told him what the doctors had said. He told me not to worry and put his hand on my throat, saying he wanted to feel for himself.

Of course, it is a little irregular to let a strange young man start touching you in this way, but he seemed so trustworthy! His hand felt very warm on my skin, and the feeling of warmth penetrated deep inside my throat. It was a very odd feeling. Then he told me it would be all right now and walked off. He barely even said goodbye. My throat immediately felt better than it had for months. I went home and tried a few scales and it was much better. I didn't know what he had done, but somehow it seemed to have helped.

When I went back to the doctors, they said that the nodules had either gone away of their own accord, or their original diagnosis had been wrong. Either way, my throat was healed, and there was no problem with it. It has been all right ever since then. I wish I could see the young man just one more time to thank him for what he did for me. My singing means everything to me, and I don't know what I would have done if I had had to stop.

SALLY
Colorado, USA

When I was in my teens, I lived with my grandparents because I didn't get along all that well with my parents. My grandmother became very ill with cancer when I was about sixteen, and as her condition worsened I spent a lot of time caring for her at home. She became very frail and we had to turn one of the ground floor rooms into a bedroom for her because she could no longer climb the stairs. She was too weak to do much at all by then. In the days leading up to her death, she was lapsing in and out of consciousness and much of what she said when conscious didn't make much sense really. I did my best to sit with her and keep her company. I didn't want her to die alone.

On the day she died, the doctor had been to see her in the morning and said that she wouldn't last much longer. She wasn't really conscious but occasionally seemed to get very agitated. I sat and held her hand, stroking it to tell her that I was there. I went to rinse out a cloth I had been wiping her forehead with, and when I came back, there was a woman standing by her bed holding her hand. People don't believe me when I tell them, but I definitely saw her. I felt almost as if I was intruding and waited outside the room for a couple of minutes. When I looked again, the woman was gone.

I went in and sat with Grandma, wiping her face with the damp cloth. She looked at me and smiled, then closed her eyes. She died about half an hour later. She still had that smile on her face. I don't know who that woman was, but I think she must have been some sort of angel sent to ease my grandma's passing.

KEVIN, 44
Bury, England

I developed an addiction to Internet chatrooms. I would be in our home office all hours of the day and night having conversations, often of a sexual nature, with strangers. I was hiding it from my wife and pretending that I was working, when in fact I was in chatrooms. She would think I was overworking and bringing too much home from the office, when in fact I was just staying up late to satisfy my urges.

Even though I recognized the symptoms of an addiction, it took me a while to react. I'd had something of a gambling addiction in my twenties, but this was different. The harm it was doing was not as immediately evident. Gambling cost me a lot of money and got me into debt, but this was eating away at my self-respect and damaging my marriage.

One night I went to bed with my wife but got up, pretending that there was some e-mail I needed to send or something. I knew she would just go back to sleep. I went down and turned on the computer. I sat there and actually felt miserable because I felt so worthless. It seemed so ridiculous that my obsession was getting me into this ridiculous subterfuge. I consciously asked in my head if there was anyone who could help me.

Then I had the strangest sensation. It was as though the room was filled with a strange presence. I felt a warmth and smelled a beautiful smell, like rose water. I felt a very urgent certainty that there was an angel there in the room. I was filled with a terrible shame at how I had been behaving. I felt that there was an angel watching me, and that it was not happy with me. I actually cried, I was so overcome by the moment, and I don't cry very often. I unplugged the computer and sat there for a long time, until I felt the presence start to fade.

For that time I had a very clear vision of how I had been harming myself and my marriage. I finally found the resolve to do something about it. The next day, I told my wife there was a problem with the computer and I pretended to take it to be repaired. In fact, I just stored it at work for a few weeks. When I brought it back home, I installed it in a different place, in the hallway right outside the bedroom, so that it was impossible to use it in any kind of secretive way.

I had a good resolve to improve my behavior, but I knew from the ways I had overcome my gambling addiction that it is important to put obstacles in your own way so that it is not so easy to slide back into bad habits. The harder it is to slip back, the less likely you are to do so. And the longer you can go without slipping back, the more the addiction is under control.

One thing that interests me about this is that although I knew for a while I was in trouble, it was only when I asked for help that help came to me. Perhaps I needed to make that mental effort to actually send out a message for help before the angel would come to me. Or perhaps it was that which alerted the angel to my state. I'm not sure, but I feel much better since I shook that addiction. Like all addictions, you have to live your life on the assumption that you are not completely healed, but I feel that the important step in moving on was made because of that angel.

BILL
Yorkshire, England

My dad told me about seeing an angel when my Uncle Gavin had died. Uncle Gav had been ill with cancer for a very long time. Eventually he was in hospital for about six weeks, sometimes conscious but mostly out of it. I was a young boy then and I remember the visits. We all tried to make sure that someone from the family visited every day, and I would go whenever my mum went along with my dad. You could tell he was very ill. He used to be a big, loud bloke, always the life and soul of any gathering. In the hospital he looked small and gray.

According to my dad, the night Uncle Gav died, Dad had gone up to the hospital to see him. His condition had worsened so they had put him in a private room and were going to call the family anyway. My dad said he got to the door of the room and, when he looked inside, Uncle Gav lay surrounded by a peaceful, glowing magical light. He didn't look as gray as he had looked; his face looked happier and more at rest.

My dad said he watched from the doorway for a while, then the light faded and he went over to Gavin. My dad insists to this day that Uncle Gav looked better. He died later that night and my dad has always been sure that he really is now at peace—he's seen it with his own eyes, he says.

Leila, 55
Copenhagen, Denmark

I work in a residential home for old people. I've seen what I believe were angels on two separate occasions. The first time was when one of our old ladies died. She had died very peacefully in the night, and I was asked to go up and make some preparations in her room because her son and daughter-in-law were on the way, having been called with the news. I walked into the room and saw there was a woman leaning over the bed with her hand on the dead lady's forehead. There was a very bright light in the room and a slightly unnatural feeling. I apologized and backed out of the room, thinking that the daughter-in-law must have arrived early.

But as I waited outside, I saw the son and daughter-in-law arrive. I had met the son before, as he was a regular visitor. We went into the room and there was no one there. I had been there the whole time and no one had come out. The woman who was there had just disappeared. That was quite strange.

The other time was different. It was with a man who had quite recently arrived. He was suffering from Alzheimer's and his children couldn't cope, so he came to us for a greater level of care. He was very difficult, as he would always be wandering off and getting confused about where he was, and he would get very angry when we tried to explain. It was upsetting to him because he had clearly been very clever and interesting in normal life, and now found it hard to cope with his own decline.

One time I went to one of the common rooms and was told that he had gone outside, and that I should go and check he was all right. I was expecting the usual difficulties, but when I got out there I saw him walking across the lawns with a younger man and a woman of about his age. The younger man was talking to him. Then he took the hand of the woman, and they walked along together very calmly.

I followed them. They went around the side of the building and, when I caught up with him, the woman and the young man were nowhere to be seen. He was the most calm and lucid I had ever seen him. He told me that he had been walking with his wife, that she had come to see him. He told me some stories about her and about how happy they had been together. He said that the young man had brought her to see him just for an hour, and that she had had to go back.

He was really serene, and seemed to know exactly where he was and what was happening. We talked for about fifteen minutes, and he was so amusing and charming, I saw him in a completely different light. I walked him back inside and then it was time for the end of my shift, so I went to say goodbye to him. He thanked me for helping him, the first time he had done anything like that since he arrived.

He died that night of a stroke. It would have been quick, which is always a blessing. I was able to check on what I had suspected: his wife had died ten years before. My belief is that an angel brought her to see him, knowing that he would soon be passing on. Perhaps the angel was helping to prepare him and her for meeting again. I'm not sure of the exact reasons, but the effect on him was remarkable, and I felt very different about him as a result. I hope that wherever he is now, he is with her and that they are very happy together.

JANE, 19
Sydney, Australia

I fell out of a tree when I was twelve. I was messing about on my own; my school had let out for the holidays a day earlier than my brothers' so I was out in the garden playing. My parents had gone out for the afternoon, leaving me alone. I tried climbing this big tree that my brothers always went up. I think I wanted to impress them by climbing it when they were there, but first I had to check if I could really do it.

I did really well, got way up farther than I expected. But then I got stuck facing forward, and I couldn't work out how to get back. For some reason, rather than wriggle backward down this big branch, I tried to turn round and go forward. That involved letting go with one hand and trying to grab the branch with the other, but I slipped and fell. It didn't look that far down as I was falling. I was just thinking how stupid I'd been. But I hit the ground really hard on my back and on the back of my head. I was pretty much knocked out cold.

I was lying on my back and I very dimly remember looking up and everything was spinning. Then I felt someone gently pushing me. I didn't see them, but I felt it—they pushed me firmly up onto my side, so I was lying looking at the tree. And then I did pass out completely, and I don't remember anything else after that.

When my parents got back, they found me there. It was another couple of hours before I woke up. I had a bit of concussion and bad bruising, but that's all. But my mother, who's done first aid courses and knows about stuff like that, said that when they found me, the first thing she noticed—apart from being scared and angry, of course—was that I was in the recovery position. And she thought to herself how lucky I was to fall and land like that. I didn't say anything about the hands I'd felt. I felt silly enough anyway, without making it worse.

SARAH, 21
Bristol, England

I got meningitis when I was fourteen. One day I felt a bit feverish, and so I left school early and went straight home. I didn't tell the teachers because it seemed like too much trouble, and I knew they'd make me wait for my mum or something. She was at work and I had a key, so I went in and laid down on the sofa. I had to draw the curtains because the light was too strong, and I drank loads of water, but then I was sick. I felt awful, but I thought it was just food poisoning or a bad cold or something.

I didn't want to call my mum because she didn't like being bothered at work. It was hard for her looking after me; she was a single parent and I'd learned to be as self-sufficient as I could possibly be. I decided to go to bed, so I tried to get up and walk to the stairs. I had all these stabbing pains when I stood up and I had to lie back down again. I was there on the sofa on my side, and I could see the phone on the other side of the room. I thought some more about phoning my mum. I'd never felt so ill, and it seemed to have gotten bad really quickly, although I still had no idea how bad it could be.

I wasn't going to call, but then I heard this voice telling me, "She won't mind." It was an actual voice, inside my head, talking out loud. It was weird. And then I still felt like I couldn't get up; I just laid there. But I felt hands on my shoulders actually pushing at me, and then holding my arm and pulling me up. I couldn't see anyone, but I definitely felt something force me up off the sofa. And then once I was upright, even though my head was hurting terribly, I was led across to the phone. I called my mum and she could hear right away how bad I was. She actually called an ambulance from work, she was so worried, and she ended up arriving home at the same time as they arrived and coming to the hospital with me.

I was ill for weeks and took a long time after that to completely recover. But they did get me onto the pills fast enough to stop it getting any worse. Now I read these stories about people dying or losing limbs or worse to the disease and I realize how very lucky I was. And it was only because I was helped. On my own I might have died. I missed a lot of school and had to take the grade over again to catch up. Mum ended up having to take time off work to help look after me, but they were very good about it and kept paying her and everything. It was bad, but it could have been a whole lot worse.

CARLA, 36
Texas, USA

I tried to kill myself a few years ago. Everything seemed hopeless and I didn't want to have to put up with it anymore. I've always been depressed, but that was the worst it's ever been. I took all my pills—I was on anti-depressants and sedatives and I took a couple of packets of each. The instructions warn you not to take more than a certain dosage so I assumed they would kill me. Actually, the drugs they give you these days are not as dangerous as the older ones; it's not so easy to take a fatal overdose, as I discovered.

I slept a long time and had very strange dreams. Then I woke up in my bed, lying on my side. I couldn't move. My throat hurt like hell because I had taken most of the pills without water and they had bruised my throat. I felt completely weird, unable to do anything, only half-awake, but very conscious of what had happened. I was worried at that point that I had done myself some terrible damage, but not enough to die. I had these terrible visions of a life in a wheelchair or hospice and felt as bad if not worse than I had the night before, when I had actually taken the pills. If I could have gotten up right then and ended it all properly I would have, but I simply couldn't.

My bedroom was up one story from the ground, but there was a roof outside my window and my curtains were open. I heard a thump and when I looked up I saw that there was a huge white cat sitting outside on the ledge. It was strange because the cat was just staring at me. It had enormous green eyes. I'd never seen it before, and that was strange as well, because there were plenty of cats in the neighborhood so it was unusual to see a different one. It didn't look like a stray. It had beautifully clean white fur, and even though it had no collar, it looked too calm and relaxed to be feral.

It sat there watching me, and I started staring back at it. It felt really strange. I felt strange anyway because of all the pills I'd taken, but staring into its eyes, I started to feel a bit calmer. I lay there for an hour or two, and the whole time the cat was staring at me. Then I fell back asleep.

I woke later, I'm not sure how much later. It was dark. The cat was still there watching me. I could see it in the light from the yard. I managed to turn the bedroom light on and stand up, but then I felt sick and had to run to the bathroom. I was sick, and when I came back with a glass of water, I was sweating and breathing heavily. The cat still sat there watching. I lay down on the floor, just inside the window, looked up at the cat, and feel back asleep.

This time I had an extremely vivid dream. The cat was there on the ledge, and it grew bigger and bigger. Then it stood up on its back feet and stretched, and it had wings. It was as tall as a man, and it was like a man, except it had a cat's face. It came inside, through the window, and came down to me on the ground. It spread its wings and folded them around me. I remember very clearly the feeling of its lovely feathers against my face and shoulders.

I felt calm and happy being held by this beautiful creature. I've always loved cats. When I was small, my parents bought me a kitten. Then it died—it got some disease. It seemed fine in the morning when I went to school, but when I came home, my parents sat me down and told me that it had died. I was devastated. And ever since, I have been worried about keeping a cat because it seems that they die so easily. But lots of my friends have them, and I always got on well with them.

I slept a long time and when I woke up, I felt a lot better. The cat was gone. I finally managed to look back on what had happened and wonder if I had been doing the right thing. I thought about my life and all that was good and bad about it, and felt that even though I had reached an absolute low, I should give it another try. I should try anything I could to make my life work again, rather than giving up. For the first time in a while, I saw life as being a sacred gift that you have to try and do what you can with.

I've always felt that that wasn't a real cat, but an angel. I think it appeared to me as a cat because I was at a stage when I simply didn't trust people. There was no kind of person who could have come to me and elicited such a positive response as that cat did. I felt that as long as it was there watching me, I was being looked after. Once I had that dream, I finally was able to reconsider all the things that had led me to being suicidal in the first place.

I still don't have a cat. When I see them, I am always reminded of what happened, but I don't think it is something that I can do. But I have changed a lot. I have ups and downs, and there are days when I wonder what it's all about. But I've never gotten as low as that again. I've realized that a lot of how I feel comes down to a basic depressive tendency that I have to put up with, but that I shouldn't make such decisions when I'm so depressed. And when I feel that bad, remembering what happened helps get me through the dark days.

PIETER, 43
Amsterdam, Holland

I think that I met my own personal guardian angel twice when I was a young boy. The first time was when I had to have an operation when I was eight years old. I'd had tonsillitis four times over the winter and, eventually, the doctor decided that the only solution was for me to have my tonsils out.

My parents took me to the hospital one evening and got me settled in my bed. I didn't like that because it was still light outside and much earlier than when I normally went to bed, and I wasn't ill, so I couldn't see why I had to put my pajamas on. Then my parents had to go and I was on my own in the ward, apart from some other sick children I didn't know and the nurses.

Everybody was very nice, but I was scared. After they put the lights out, a boy about my own age came over to my bed and asked if I was having my tonsils out. I told him that I was. He said that he'd had his done two days before. I asked him if it hurt and he said that it didn't at the time because you were asleep, but that it was a bit sore afterward.

Then he said that he hadn't minded his throat being sore because you got as much ice cream as you wanted. I was already feeling much better about my operation when he put his hand on my forehead. I remember that very clearly, firstly because it's not something that young boys do, but more importantly because his hand was wonderfully cool and a little damp. That doesn't sound very nice when I say it, but it felt like someone had put a block of ice cream, just out of the freezer, onto my head and, to me, it was the most calming and wonderful sensation.

I must have fallen asleep and I can't recall the next morning or the anesthetic or anything. The next thing I remember is waking up and feeling like I'd swallowed barbed wire. What was a bit strange is that the first person I saw was the boy from the night before. He asked me if I'd had any ice cream yet, and I tried to answer but I couldn't talk, so I just shook my head. He said he'd go and ask the nurse if I could have some, but before he went he put out his hand again and this time he rested it on my throat. You'd think that if a stranger did that you might panic, but I completely trusted him and I felt that wonderful coolness flow into me again. My throat stopped hurting in an instant and I started to drift off just as the boy went away to find the nurses. He didn't come back, but I got my ice cream.

I didn't see him again until I got knocked off my bike by a car about three years later. The driver stopped and helped me up, but he didn't stick around and check that I was really okay. Just after he'd driven off, a boy of, again, about my own age came up to me and picked up my bike. He said that he thought I might have broken my arm, and that we should get back to my house and wait for my mum to get home from work. It was only a short walk to the house, and he pushed my bike and chattered about nothing much while I held my arm in my other hand to try and stop it hurting. I didn't know how he knew where I lived, and I didn't know how he knew my arm was broken, and I didn't know who he was until we got to my house.

I was trying to get my key out of my pocket, but my arm was too painful to let down and he gently held it for me. That wonderful cold, soothing sensation that I'd always remembered flowed into my arm and it stopped hurting. I suddenly realized that he was the boy from the hospital, but before I could say anything, my mum's car pulled up and he said goodbye and ran off. It occurred to me then that he also seemed to know that my mum was due back from work, when there was no reason at all that he should have.

Anyway, she took me to the hospital, and my arm, which was of course broken, got plastered. She spent the whole journey home in a fury with me because I couldn't remember the license plate number of the car that had knocked me down. I didn't mind. My arm never hurt the whole time and I knew I had my own personal guardian angel that would show up if I needed him. It's a great feeling.

NERYS, 56
Maine, USA

I got pneumonia once when I was staying in Manhattan. It was ironic because it was a really hot June, but I caught it from the air conditioning. Apparently it's quite a common cause. You come in out of the heat into this cold air, and if your lungs are a bit weakened by a cold or infection, you just start getting water on the lungs.

I felt worse and worse and then I fainted in Macy's and ended up in the hospital. They were very good and diagnosed me right away. I spent a couple of nights there, quite ill, on heavy antibiotics. Then on the third day, I felt a bit better and asked if I could leave. The doctors were quite doubtful and made me sign all kinds of disclaimers. They also wanted to know if I had someone to look after me, and I said I did, even though I didn't. Clearly I wasn't okay.

I suppose it was a bit pig-headed of me. I was just so sick of the hospital and I felt better, so I thought I'd be fine. I was staying at the New Yorker Hotel, near Penn Station. By the time I got there in the taxi, I was feeling really weak and already realizing I'd probably been a bit too keen to get out. It was quite surreal because it was this beautiful weather outside. I was up on the twentieth floor with a lovely view out over Manhattan and the river, and the room was sweltering hot because I'd had to turn off the air conditioning so it wouldn't make me worse. And I just lay there in bed, looking out at the view, sweating and shivering.

I passed out more than fell asleep. All night I was feverish and my chest hurt terribly. I took as many painkillers as I could and still I felt terrible. Along toward dawn, I was drifting in and out of sleep and having strange dreams. The thing I remember is that every time I started to fall asleep or woke up, I saw the room as it was, but with two shimmering figures, one either side of my bed. Their faces were impassive. They looked half-real, as though they were partly in this world and partly somewhere else.

Every time I woke up I saw them there, and then they melted away as I woke up properly, and every time I fell asleep, they were the last thing I saw before I went to sleep. I'm not sure if they were helping me, or if they were simply there, visible to me, because I was so ill. The next day I was still in a terrible fever, but I managed to eat a bit and make it through the day. That night was exactly the same, with the vision of the two angels there constant throughout the night.

The day after that I managed to get up. I went back to the hospital, and without exactly saying "I told you so," they pointed out that I was actually worse than when I'd checked myself out. They gave me some injections and kept me in for another couple of days. I stopped seeing the figures then, and finally started to get better.

I always wonder who they were. Did they come because I was ill, or are they always there but invisible to me? I guess I'll never know, not in this life anyway.

ALISON, 47
Manchester, England

I was addicted to sleeping pills and painkillers a few years ago. I wasn't very happy at the time, and I had been using more and more drugs to try and make myself better, but really it was only making things worse. I had enough sense to realize I was harming myself and I resolved to give them up. But rather than cut down gradually, I decided that the only way was to stop them all immediately. I tipped a few bottles of pills down the sink and threw out all the packets in one go.

I realized later that this was quite risky and foolhardy. Any doctor seeing what I was taking would have recommended that I go off the drugs gradually. The withdrawal effects, particularly from the sleeping pills, were quite bad. I started to get fluttery heart rhythms and hot flushes. My blood pressure was very low and I would get unpredictably dizzy when I stood up. I don't suppose it's anything like as bad as the withdrawal from more serious drug addictions, but it was pretty unpleasant nonetheless.

After two days, I felt a little better and went out to the market, but I started to feel terrible while I was there. I was extremely pale and sweating profusely, and I felt like I might faint. I sat down on a low wall, just so I wouldn't faint. At that moment, a man passed with a tray of jewelry he was about to set up and start selling. He stopped beside me and started rummaging around inside a shoulder bag. He brought out a little golden angel figure and gave it to me. He said, "I think you'll need this. If you're feeling bad, hold on to it." And then he just kept walking.

I had nothing to lose, so I held the angel in my hand. Gradually my heart stopped racing and I started to feel a bit better. After that, every time I felt bad, I took the angel out and held it until I felt better, and it really seemed to be helping me somehow. It took a few weeks before the symptoms really went away, and it was a difficult time, but the angel helped. Whenever I held it, I had an image in my head of a big angel figure that just held me in its arms and rocked me from side to side until I felt okay. I found that very soothing.

I went to the doctor later on and told him what I'd done. He said that, while he was very pleased that I had managed to get off the medication, I'd been a bit stupid to do it without medical supervision—which is probably true, but at least I had a bit of help along the way.

MARTIN
Toronto, Canada

My father was diagnosed with cancer of the throat when he was in his sixties. It got quite bad and he was having trouble eating and swallowing. He was on medication and the medication made him feel bad as well. He was very stoic about it, but you could tell he wasn't happy. He had smoked a pipe all his life and he hated the fact that he had to give it up. He'd always enjoyed his food and drink so having those kinds of pleasures taken away from him was very difficult.

I hated it when he was ill. He had always seemed so independent and strong, and now he seemed weak and tired. There were difficult moments, such as when he would try to eat a meal and end up being sick. It was horrible for all of us. I believe he felt humiliated as well as unwell.

One day he came home looking very happy and told me a strange thing. He said that he had been in the hospital waiting room, waiting for his consultation, when he had met an old man who said he knew a bit about cancer. The man had asked if he could feel his throat. Now my father had no patience for any kind of New Age healing or alternative medicine. But he let this man place his hands on his throat. He said there was a strange warmth that came from his hands. Then the man told him that he would be more comfortable now, and not to worry too much.

That day my father ate a much better meal than he had for months. He seemed much better. The day after and the day after that, it was the same. I asked him if he thought the treatment was working. He said no, he thought the treatment was a waste of time. He said he was dying and that it was only a matter of time, but that all he could hope for was to be as comfortable as possible.

That's a very hard thing to hear from your father, but I suppose it was his way of coping. He hated false sentimentality and irrationality, and he reacted to illness with the same approach as everything in his life. But he was much better for weeks after he saw that man at the hospital. He didn't talk about it much, but the one other time he mentioned it, he said that whoever he was, he knew a few things that the doctors didn't. He was quite comfortable that month, and was very talkative and cheerful. When he'd been bad, he had withdrawn into himself a bit, but now he was full of fun and told me lots of anecdotes about his life and my childhood that I hadn't heard before.

When he died, it was very unexpected. He was watching ice hockey, something he'd always enjoyed. He'd had a good meal that night and he was pretty happy. Then, just after the end of the match, he had a stroke right there in his chair. It was just like falling asleep. He looked quite happy. It's never good when someone close to you dies, but there are good and bad ways to go, and I think he had a pretty good way. I'm very grateful that that last month was so good, and wonder if it was an angel helping out that gave us that little bit of extra time with him at his best.

JANET
Melbourne, Australia

I used to get terrible migraines. I think it was a reaction to stress, but at the time anything seemed to set them off—red wine, tea, bright lights, chocolate, you name it. There was nothing I could do when I got them except go and lie down in a darkened room. The pain was terrible and any movement made me feel sick and dizzy.

One time I was out shopping when one started to come on. I could feel it building from my temples and gradually starting to take hold. I was upset because I didn't know where I could go. I put down my basket and just walked out of the shop to look for a place to lie down, or maybe a taxi to take me home. But outside it was terrible; the sunlight was far too bright and there was noise and people moving around everywhere. I really thought I might faint from the pain, and I was panicking about what to do.

Then a woman walked up to me out of the crowd and said not to worry, she'd look after me. She took my arm and led me back into the shop and into a far corner, where there was a bed I could lie down on. She looked a bit like me, but maybe a bit younger. She kept telling me not to worry, and then she put her hands on either side of my face, with her fingers on my temples. She said she could make me better. I felt all the tension and pain flowing out of my body. It was incredible.

When I woke up, there was a crowd of people all around me in the sunlight. I had actually fainted and fallen on the sidewalk. I'd hit my head and people were worried that I had hurt myself. My head did hurt a bit where I'd banged it, but the migraine was completely gone. It was a miracle, almost—extraordinary, anyway.

I never get migraines any more. I sometimes feel the start of one, but I just stay calm and put my fingers to my temples, like the woman or angel did, and I feel the pain draining away.

HALE, 56
New York, USA

This is something that I witnessed in the late seventies. It was in the meatpacking district in Manhattan, outside one of those clubs that used to come and go up and down the West Side. It was very rough around there then, and I usually had the sense to make sure I left with a friend, but on this occasion, my friend had gone off with a girl and there was no one else I knew.

I started walking over toward Tenth Avenue when I heard gunshots. I had no idea where they had come from, so I ran in the direction that I thought was away from the shots. But it turned out to be a wrong guess, and I nearly got knocked down by a big car that came shooting round the corner off Tenth. I ran around the corner in the opposite direction, and in front of me there was a NYPD car and a small crowd of people on the pavement.

I got some of the story that night, and some later, but to simplify things, a cop had pulled over the car that had nearly run me down, for some minor reason, but the guy was wanted in a serious way, so he just shot first before the cop could work out who he was. The cop, who was out of his car, was hit twice, in the leg and shoulder. It's terrible that something like that should happen to someone who's only doing his job.

At the time, all I knew for sure was that the cop had been shot and was lying there on the pavement in a pool of blood. There was a lot of blood. There were a few people standing around, panicking or not knowing what to do. Someone had already called the NYPD, so they were on the way.

A tall man walked up just as I got there. He knelt down on the ground next to the cop and put his hands over his leg. He stayed there like that and calmly asked someone if there was help coming. They said there was, and he nodded and sighed, as though this was a sad thing, but the kind of thing he saw all the time. It was strange. At the time, I wondered if he was a doctor or something. But he didn't examine the cop or anything, just held his leg tightly in his hands. I stayed, mainly because I didn't know what else to do, and also because I figured they might need a description of the car, so I should give the cops my number.

When the medical team got there, the man stayed holding him like that and spoke to one of the team. I didn't hear it at the time, but afterward the story was that he told them that the cop was shot in the artery and they had to keep holding the wound to keep him from bleeding too heavily. The thing is, they would have worked that out for themselves soon enough, but he couldn't afford to lose much more blood. The man saved him firstly by stemming the flow of blood, and secondly by promptly alerting the medics to his condition. They might otherwise have started by treating the shoulder wound, which looked worse, and missed the leg wound for long enough for him to die. The shoulder wound looked bad, but the bullet had gone straight through and didn't hit any major blood vessels, so by itself it wasn't life-threatening.

I talked to the cops and they took my name, and then we all drifted away, leaving this bloodstain on the pavement. The stain was still visible when I walked by two weeks later. There was an appeal on the radio; they said that the man who had helped the cop must have been a doctor who was passing, otherwise he would never have had the knowledge to know what to do. But no one seemed to be able to describe him clearly, including me. I just had an impression of his features, but couldn't remember his face. I knew for sure he hadn't done any kind of medical examination. The cop got a medal, and he deserved it for what he had gone through, but the stranger who had saved him never claimed any reward or credit.

Of course he never told anyone who he was, and everyone forgot about it in the end. But who else but an angel could have walked up like that, seen a man covered in blood with two separate wounds, and known exactly what to do without even looking, and which wound to treat? No man could have done that. And the crowd of us there, no matter how scared we were and how much we wanted to help, would probably have just put him in the recovery position and prayed for the best. He apparently only just saved the cop's life, even then. A minute more, without any help, and the cop probably would have been gone.

I don't call it a miracle. I call it a revelation, or an intervention. The angel must have either known exactly what was going to happen, or he must have been there ready to help when the guy needed it most.

MAX, 36
California, USA

About ten years ago, I was going through a very bad period. I was having anxiety attacks where I couldn't breathe properly, and I'd start to get dizzy, with my heart pounding away. It was because of all the mess I was in, in my life. I had been stealing money at work to try and pay off my debts. I had been doing too many drugs—mostly amphetamines—and also, while I was out of my head, I had been sleeping around, mostly unsafe sex, and this was at the peak of the spread of AIDS. I'm not a particularly bad person, but I'd been behaving in a very irresponsible and foolish way for too long. I was in so many different kinds of trouble I didn't know where to start worrying. I'd try to put it all out of my head, but then I would just get the anxiety attacks from trying to push it away.

One particularly bad day, I went for a walk down into town. I went into a coffee bar to sit for a while. The place was empty, but then one other person came in, a woman of about my mother's age. She bought herself a coffee and came to sit at the table next to mine, even though there was plenty of empty space. She looked at me and asked if I was all right. I said I was fine, but she just kept talking. She said she could see I wasn't all right. And to be fair, I was sweating and shaking badly. I'd been sitting there muttering to myself, so anyone could have seen that I wasn't in the best shape.

Without being invited, she moved from the table she was sitting at to the table opposite me. She asked me what

I was worrying about, and I told her that I was worrying about so many things I wouldn't know where to start worrying. But she insisted, and after a moment of resisting, I found myself telling her everything, even about the drugs and the stealing. There was no reason for me to do this, but I just trusted her. She had such a calm, sensible face, and nothing I said seemed to shock her. In fact, nothing I said even seemed to surprise her. It was as though she already knew everything about me, but just needed me to tell her myself.

It was a great relief to me to tell someone all this stuff. She didn't give me a great deal of advice. Mostly she told me that these were my problems and I had to work out what to do about them myself. But she did two things that made a real difference. First she told me to write a list and to think about each problem in isolation. She told me I was getting them all mixed up and thinking there were no solutions, simply because there wasn't one big solution. She was right about that. I'd been getting to the point where I was considering running away, getting out of the country to try to start all over again because it all seemed such a mess.

Then she did a simple thing. She took my hand and told me that when I was getting anxious, to remember her and stay calm. She told me that should be my mantra until I made at least some of my problems better. I should stop myself from panicking by saying "calm, calm, calm" in my head. While she told me this, she was holding my hand, and this was the most mystical thing about the conversation. I could feel her strength flowing into me as she spoke. There was a kind of warmth that started in my hand and spread right through me. I could feel myself calming down even as we talked. Then she told me again that it was up to me, and left. I realized I wanted to ask her more questions so I ran after her, just after she went through the door, but she was gone. So I went back to my coffee. I could still feel her warmth on the back of my hand.

I did exactly what she said. It's not often that someone can have such an impact on you, but on this occasion I just knew that she was a messenger of some kind in my life, and that I was being given a real opportunity. I separated all the problems out in my mind and dealt with each in turn. I stopped stealing and took on extra work to try and clear my debts. I stopped taking the drugs, which helped a lot with money, and I got myself tested for HIV (happily it was negative; I could easily have been less lucky).

Gradually the anxiety attacks started to go away. Every time I got anxious about money, or found myself wanting to go off my head and do something stupid, I remembered her holding my hand and I made myself be calm like she had said. To this day, I can close my eyes if I have a problem and feel the warmth and strength of her hand on mine, as though she is still there.

Don't get me wrong; I didn't become a saint overnight. It wasn't a total religious conversion, because that just isn't me. But from a low point in my life, I learned how to improve my life little by little, and how to be more considerate and reasonable in my behavior, and I think that made a real difference to my life. In a way, I think that she may have been there more for the sake of the people around me, people I was hurting, than she was for me in particular. I didn't really deserve her help, but by helping me she helped others too.

ROGER, 54
Liverpool, England

I think I once saw an angel at an accident scene on the other side of the road. I do a lot of driving as part of my job; I'm a sales rep for a medical supplies company on Merseyside. I was halfway through a long journey a few months ago when all the traffic on the motorway started to slow right down. It's not unusual for that to happen, and it's usually for no reason and everything picks up again a few miles on. Sometimes it's roadworks and occasionally, unfortunately, it's because there's been an accident in the opposite lanes and people are slowing down to see what's going on. I don't know why they do it; it's pretty ghoulish, and I always try not to look. This time, the cars in front of me had come to an almost complete stop just as I was opposite the place where the accident had happened. I couldn't help glancing over. It looked as if a car and a motorbike had hit each other.

The car was dented and in the middle of the lane, and the bike was lying on its side about thirty yards away. An ambulance was there, and a couple of people who seemed a bit shaken up, with blankets around their shoulders, were standing next to it. I presumed that they had been in the car and they didn't look as if they'd been badly hurt. The motorcyclist was lying on a stretcher in the road, still with his helmet on, while one of the paramedics was doing something to the neck brace they'd put him in, and what I thought was another paramedic was crouched beside the stretcher.

I couldn't quite make out his features, even though I was pretty close. I thought for a minute that there must still have been some smoke drifting around from the collision, but when I looked to see where it might be coming from, I realized that there wasn't any smoke at all. The first paramedic went over to the ambulance, and I was able to see that the other one was more like a misty shape than a solid person. He seemed to be somehow lit from inside his body. I actually did that thing of closing my eyes and pinching myself, wondering if I'd had too much coffee, but when I looked again the figure was still there with his hand on the motorcyclist's forehead.

Just then, the paramedic came back with his partner who, apparently, had been looking after the people from the car. They lifted the stretcher and started to take it to the ambulance. The motorcyclist reached out his hand to the misty figure, and the paramedics, who were clearly not aware of any other presence, tried to make him put it down.

It was all right, though, because the figure—which I was by now sure was an angel—stayed alongside the injured man, even though he didn't really seem to move. I was just able to see the stretcher go into the ambulance, with the angel right next to it, when the traffic started to move forward again. The last thing I saw was the light from the angel filling the interior of the ambulance as the doors closed. As I drove off, instead of feeling a bit sick, like I normally do when I see an accident, I felt oddly happy and sure that the motorcyclist would recover, however badly hurt he might have been. I'm certain that there was an angel taking care of him.

MATTHEW, 59
London, England

I saw a man die in a car accident once. It was on a road near to where I live. I saw the whole thing. He walked out at the same time as a blue car came out of a side road, far too fast. He was holding a mobile phone, and I suppose he was distracted, but the driver was at fault. The driver didn't even stop. He must have known what happened, because the man went up onto the windscreen and was thrown onto the pavement. But the driver just accelerated and drove away. Someone got the license plates, but the car was found abandoned later. It was probably someone dodgy, without insurance, so they couldn't track him down.

The man who had been hit was lying there on the pavement. He had been hit hard in the hip and torso and had hit his head hard on the pavement when he landed. There were about five of us there and we all ran over. A few drivers stopped as well. Someone called an ambulance. It was a horrible situation. My heart was beating fast with adrenaline, but I wasn't sure what to do. No one else knew what to do, either. Obviously none of us knew much about first aid, but I did know that it was a bad idea to move him if he had head or neck injuries. I was asking him how he was, and he looked up at me as though he was conscious, but he couldn't talk. I honestly thought he would be all right once the ambulance got there. He wasn't bleeding or obviously wounded, even though he had hit his head. It didn't seem like the sort of thing that could kill you, but I suppose these things are a matter of luck.

We were just all standing there, feeling impotent because we couldn't help. Then this girl walked past me. She was quite young and didn't look like she was from the area. She just knelt down beside him and started to stroke his hair. She leaned down and whispered in his ear, and he smiled at her. She was there for about a minute doing that as we all watched. She wasn't doing any first aid or anything, just comforting him and whispering to him. And it seemed to help.

Then he gave a big shudder and closed his eyes. The girl stood up and said that he was dead. She didn't check his pulse or breathing. She just calmly said it, and she apologized to us, saying she was sorry we'd been there and not to worry, we couldn't have helped him. I remember that she was very calm and seemed to know for a fact that he was dead and that there was nothing anyone could have done. Then the ambulance arrived and people started running around. Someone was asking me about the crash and if I'd seen the driver. When I looked around for the girl, she was gone.

Looking back, it was a very strange scene, the five of us standing around and her just stroking his hair like that. If she had been a doctor or nurse or something, I feel like she would have been doing checks on him. But it was as though she knew he was dying, and all she could do was comfort and soothe him. And she seemed to succeed in doing that.

Personally, I think she was the angel who came for him when he died, and that after he died she escorted him to somewhere else. That may be too much of an assumption on my part, but she looked like an angel and didn't behave like any person I've ever met. You would think that even if angels can't rescue you from death, they might be there to meet you when you go.

It's partly seeing someone die in front of you, and partly the strangeness of the girl, but I found myself seeing life very differently after that experience. I felt much more aware that we could die at any time, but also less scared of it than I used to be.

WHEN ANGELS
INTERVENE

I debated long and hard about which accounts to include
in this chapter. Many of the stories in other chapters
could easily have been placed here instead, while some
may feel that accounts such as those of Mathieu and
Thomas are simply coincidental rescues rather than genuine angelic encounters. In the end, I included the latter
in part because the people who told me these stories were
genuine in their belief and honest in their accounts, even
where they told me about their uncertainties and doubts.
Thomas seems genuinely unsure what happened in his
rescue from fire, but he has been touched by that rescue
nonetheless in a way that informs his everyday life. In
all these cases, I think that there is a possibility that the
accounts are of genuine angelic intervention. But if you
conclude that they are merely stories of humans helping

other humans, the very least that one can say is that these stories show humans at their most angelic.

MATHIEU, 40
Lyon, France

This happened on the housing estate where I grew up, when I was ten years old. The area was a bit industrial; we used to play in the old warehouses and in the ruins of ones that had been knocked down. It was probably all a bit dangerous, but we were kids, we didn't care. There were never any grown-ups around. There was a canal out the back where you could go and play. It was not a picturesque canal, just a bit of industrial wasteland really.

One day an eight-year-old kid I knew was there, and he was looking after his little brother, who was about four, not much more than a toddler. I had seen them earlier throwing stones in the canal, and I was quite close by when it happened. I heard the eight-year-old (I've forgotten his name) come shouting that his brother was in the canal. The younger boy had seen a patch of weeds floating on the surface and it looked so dense he thought he could step onto it. Before the older brother knew what had happened, the kid had plunged into the deep water, and he couldn't swim so his brother was desperate, panicking.

I ran as fast as I could. I could swim and, even though it was not very safe, I would have jumped in and tried to help. You can't let a four-year-old drown. But when I got there, there was a big commotion in the water, and a man surfaced holding the kid. He heaved him over the edge and then knelt down over him. He was covered in green weed. His clothes would be ruined. He knelt and pumped at the kid's chest until he heaved up all this mucky water, canal bilge, onto the bank. Then the man gave him artificial respiration. The boy jerked and started breathing. The man told us to carry him back to his mother's house and not to let him play near the water again. (There was no need for this; both of them were terrified of water for a long time afterward.)

We ran off without thinking to look to see where the man went, and no one ever found out who he was or why he was passing. I'm inclined to see it as a miraculous event. The one and only time I remember someone falling in, there happened to be a stranger passing, someone we had never seen before, even though this was a remote neighborhood, rarely frequented by strangers. It is too unlikely to be chance; there must have been more to it.

Thomas, 32
London, England

A few years ago I lived in a place where there was a bad fire. It was a terrible building, run by landlords who just didn't care. I was put there because I was homeless at the time, and I was grateful for a bed, but even I could see that the place was run by crooks. The stairs often didn't have lights, there were four stories of bedsits, and all the places where there should have been fire extinguishers were empty. Inevitably someone managed to start a fire, probably falling asleep drunk with a cigarette.

I was woken at three in the morning by a lot of shouting and the smell of smoke. I grabbed my dressing gown and ran to the door. The handle was a little hot, and when I opened it a crack there was rush of flames toward me, and intense heat. Obviously the hallway and the stairs were alight, and that was the only way out of my flat. I was on the third floor, so jumping was out of the question, but I decided I had to try to go out the window. This was all happening very fast. Already I could feel the air getting very hot and thin, and I thought it was only a matter of time before my place went up. I heard some terrible screaming somewhere. A couple people did die in that fire, and I still have nightmares about what it must have been like for them.

I actually had to smash the window to get out. It had been painted shut by the idiot landlords, so couldn't be opened properly. I managed to do it with a chair and knocked most of the glass out, although I still got some cuts climbing through it. There was a drainpipe that I could just reach, and I kind of slid and clambered down to a sloping roof a story below me. From there, I had no way down except to jump. It was at the back of the building, so I would be jumping into a disused yard where the old furniture got dumped. There wasn't enough light to see clearly where I was landing, so it was very dangerous. I could have stayed there, and for a while I thought I should wait to be rescued. But then flames started coming through the walls and roof, only about twenty yards away, and the roof I was standing on was making terrible noises and getting hotter.

Then, from down below, I heard a man shouting to me. I could just make out his pale face looking up at me. He shouted that I should jump, he'd catch me. It seemed a lunatic idea, but he shouted again, and then I thought there was nothing else for it. Otherwise I was going to die there. So I shouted "I'm coming" and he said "Yes, now." I jumped and fell all that way, and he was there. I felt him catch me and break the fall. It must have hurt him because I had fallen a long way. He dropped me, but he had broken my fall enough that I survived. I broke a leg—it twisted sideways—and I knocked my head so that I was half-conscious. The man picked me up and carried me away, out of that backyard and round the corner to the main road. There were about four fire engines there and a couple of ambulances, and one of them took me to hospital, still half-conscious, in pain from my leg but alive.

The local paper covered the story in some detail, partly because they wanted to do an exposé of the bad landlords who ran the place. I told them about the man who saved me so they ran a story about the hero rescuer, and offered a reward, but no one ever came forward. None of the hospitals seemed to have treated anyone for the kind of injuries he must have suffered for catching an adult male who had fallen from that height.

I've never really known what to think. When I read about angels, it seems to me to be the only explanation. How would anyone else even have known I was there, let alone managed to break my fall? Or maybe it was just an amazing person, someone so heroic he managed to save my life and didn't feel the need to take the credit. I can't work it out, but I know I owe my life to somebody, and I try to remember that every day and live my life accordingly.

CHEIKO
Tokyo, Japan

I had just split up with my college boyfriend and was feeling a bit down. I went to a café/bar and sat reading a book and drinking a beer. Another customer came in and seemed to be looking for someone. When she saw me, she asked if she could join me, as if it was me she had been looking for all along. I said she was welcome to sit down and wondered if I had met her before. She seemed familiar to me and I felt comfortable with her, as you do when among old friends. We chatted about this and that until it was getting fairly late.

I said that I had better be going and she asked me which route I took home. The area of Tokyo I live in has lots of alleyways, and the quickest way to my apartment block was through these alleys involving a lot of twists and turns. The girl seemed to grow worried when I told her my way home and asked me to accompany her as far as the subway station. From the station my route home would be along a street lined with shops. Finally I agreed to go with her via the station. At the station entrance, we swapped phone numbers and I carried on home.

The next day on the news, I learned that a notorious criminal, who had been attacking young girls and who was being hunted by the police, was caught hiding in the alleyways near my place. Had I gone home that way, he could have attacked me. Feeling a little strange about this, I looked for the phone number the girl had given me the previous night. I called it, but got a recording that said the number did not exist. I called the telephone company and tried to get her number from her name, but she didn't exist on their records, either. I never saw her again, but I'm sure she was some sort of angel sent to protect me that night.

John
Cardiff, Wales

I work as a long-distance truck driver. I'm often away from home for days at a time and tend to get home very late at night or in the early hours of the morning. One very cold November night, I had just finished my shift and was driving home. It would have been about 11:30, and it was freezing cold and a bit foggy. Suddenly, in front of me was a woman waving her arms about, to get me to stop. I pulled over to the side of the road and got out. A girl was lying in the road, obviously injured and in quite a bad way.

The woman told me the girl had been the victim of a hit-and-run and asked if I had a phone. I did and called an ambulance after getting the girl's name and age from the woman. I waited with them until the ambulance arrived.

As they carried the girl inside, I found out which hospital they were taking her to so that I could find out later whether she was okay.

About a week later, I received a card from her parents, thanking me for helping to save their daughter's life. I went to see the girl and told her that the woman she had been with was the one who had really saved her. The girl looked puzzled and said that she had been walking home from a party alone when the accident happened. There had been no woman with her. I don't normally believe in such things, but that woman was definitely there and she was intent on getting help for the girl. It must have been the work of an angel.

JANE
Newcastle, England

My husband and I were on a driving holiday in Scotland when we decided we were lost. I had been the map reader and tensions were high. My husband was getting very angry with me. His face was turning red and he kept punching the steering wheel. There were no landmarks around us, just the moors and mountains. A misty fog was starting to come down from the mountains and we thought we might be forced to spend the night in the car without food or water.

Suddenly a very tall man appeared, seemingly out of nowhere, and we opened the car window to ask him for directions. He gave us very detailed directions to the nearest pub where they offered bed and breakfast. We were so grateful that we offered to drive him wherever he was going. He said a funny thing that I will always remember: "You can't get to where I'm going by car." He just set off down the road and we watched him go. Whatever he was or wherever he was going, he definitely saved us that day.

JAMES
Leeds, England

When I was a young lad, the shop on the corner of our street burned down. I remember waking up in the middle of the night to all the yelling and shouting and the sound from the fire engines. My mum and dad were up and dressed and most of the neighbors were out in the street.

An old lady called May ran the shop. She was lovely to us kids, always giving us the odd penny candy for free. I watched the firemen put a ladder to the front of her shop and climb up with the hose. They were very busy putting out the fire. I saw one of them come out of May's backyard with May over his shoulder, carrying her just like you see on TV. He put her on the ground on a blanket and someone called for the ambulance.

The rest of the firemen put out the fire but the place was a ruin. One of them came over to my dad and said he was sorry they hadn't managed to get into the building to save May; the fire had caught hold very quickly and the building had been too hot and unsafe for any of the men to go in. My dad said that we'd all watched one of the firemen bring her out of the back. The fireman looked puzzled and went over to ask the rest of their crew who had been inside. The thing was, none of them had. But we all saw the fireman carry her out. He had the uniform on and everything.

May recovered and went on to live another fifteen years and have three great-grandchildren. The story of the unknown "angel" fireman who saved her life is told around those streets to this day.

BILL
West Virginia, USA

I was working for the fire department when a tornado announcement came through. It was about 11:15 a.m. and we had to get to the school to get the children to safety in the basement. The crew arrived at school with only minutes to spare, but found that the children had already been led to safety.

The school principal, Mrs. Adosi, told the men that some police officers had come by the school earlier to tell them to go to the basement. We later found out that the children had been led to safety a quarter-hour before the fire department got the tornado warning. The local police station had not been involved. Who looked after those children? We don't know. Angels? I'd say that was far-fetched, but certainly someone looked after those kids that day.

PATRICK, 29
London, England

When I was sixteen or seventeen, I was hanging around with a bad crew in Hackney. It was a poor area where I grew up, not that I mean that as an excuse. But we hated all the yuppies that were moving in. That was our excuse, but if it wasn't that, it would have been someone else, foreigners or whatever. We just had too much hatred and energy in us. We used to go out on the weekend and find people to beat up. A gang of six of us. The leader was a kid called Cass, who was really just a psycho; we were all scared of him. Anything crazy anyone else would do, he'd do it ten times as bad.

One Friday about 10:00 p.m. it was the same as usual, six of us hanging around a few streets away from where we live, looking for someone to pick on. This yuppie type came round the corner, in his suit with a briefcase. He was more of a trendy arts type than a proper business-man, but he obviously had money. We faced up to him and Cass demanded his bag. He gave him that, no question—you could see he was scared. But then we started laying into him anyway. No reason; that was just what we did. It's hard to justify looking back, but at the time I just thought it was what kids did at the weekend. He was just someone to hate. I could have passed him in the street next day and not cared, but when we were all there, up for a fight, it had to be him.

He was on the floor, covering his face with his arms, and we'd all stopped hitting him except Cass, who kept kicking him and telling him to get up and fight. That was when I saw two men standing beyond him, about twenty yards away, just staring at us.

I shouted something at them. Told them to get away or something. Dave, who was one of my mates, asked who I was shouting at and I realized that no one else could see them, just me. They were watching me. Both of them had these sad expressions on their faces, but the one on the left stared straight at me and looked angry. And for the first time ever, I felt ashamed of what we were doing. Suddenly I could see how it looked, the six of us picking on some poor bloke who couldn't defend himself. It felt pretty bad to realize suddenly what a terrible thing I was doing.

The two men looked at me one more time and walked off down the road. For some reason, I knew I had to go after them. I just mumbled something and ran off after them. They turned a corner and I followed, then I could see them at the end of the road, too far away. By the time I got to that corner, they were gone.

I went home and had a bath and spent the whole weekend thinking about what had happened. Cass called round but I told him I was ill. I could hardly look him in the face. The week after that, I basically ran away from home. I took my stuff and went way off to the other side of town where I didn't know anyone. I didn't have much money, but luckily I found a job washing dishes and managed to get a cheap place to stay. I turned my life round completely, and started to try different things and make different kinds of friends. Looking back, it is unbelievable what I was like then. I used to go back and see my mum, but I never went to see any of those friends again. I don't know what they thought happened to me. I suppose I could have tried to persuade them to change their ways as well, but they never would have. It's just not like that.

I heard a few years ago that Cass was in prison for attempted murder. He was into gangs and all that, so it was inevitable. It probably would have been the same for me if I hadn't managed to get away. So far as I'm concerned, those two men were definitely angels.

KAREN, 27
Northampton, England

When I first started teaching, I found a job in a primary school in North London. I'd been quite nervous about how I'd cope with real teaching, on my own in a classroom for the first time, but mostly it was a lot of fun and very rewarding.

The only time I had a real problem was on Fridays, when I used to have a different class for the last hour of the day. My class used to go off to the playground or the gym with the teacher who taught physical education, and I'd cover his class while that happened. I didn't have to do anything special. I didn't even have to prepare a lesson plan or anything; it was just supervised reading. I'd help them with difficult spellings, and we'd sometimes read aloud.

But they were a really difficult group of children, noisy and rude, and I just couldn't seem to keep them under control. They were a bit older than my class, ten or eleven years old, but they seemed much older and they often actually frightened me. I know it sounds stupid, but I started to dread that end-of-the-week humiliation and I'd start worrying about it from Tuesday onward.

I mentioned it once to the physical education teacher, and he said to yell at them a bit and they'd calm down. But when I tried that, most of them ignored me and a few of them started imitating me, which got the rest of them laughing. It was horrible. It was affecting me so much that I knew I wasn't doing as good a job as I should have been with my own class, and I started to seriously consider giving up teaching altogether. I know now that, with any class, Friday afternoons can sometimes be a bit tricky, but back then I just thought that I wasn't up to the job.

One Friday, just before the Easter holiday, I burst into tears on my way in to work and had to stop the car and try and get myself together. I decided that I'd teach the class today for the last time and then go and see the head teacher and tell him that I wasn't coping. I knew that he'd probably tell me that coping was what I was being paid for. I expected to have to resign.

I don't remember what I did with my own class that day; I only remember wishing them a happy Easter, carefully not mentioning that they'd probably have a new teacher when they got back from their holiday. They all said "Happy Easter, Miss" in that sing-song way that children do when they all speak together, and I nearly cried again.

When I got to the physical education teacher's classroom in the afternoon, a boy that I didn't know was standing outside the door. He said that he was Kevin Ritchie's
cousin, and that he was staying with the Ritchies over
Easter because his parents were visiting his grandmother,
who was ill. Kevin was in my class, but he hadn't mentioned it and I said so. The boy said that he'd had a note
from Kevin's parents, but that he'd already given it to the
physical education teacher. It wasn't unknown for this
sort of thing to happen, although the visiting child would
normally go to the same class as their relative, so I just
accepted it—I think I was too distracted to do anything
else. I didn't even bother asking his name.

All the rest of the kids were already in the classroom
and, when we went in, the boy sat down next to a nasty,
fat bully who I shall call Jono (in case his parents read
this). I told them to get out their books and, straight
away, Jono started chanting "boring, boring, boring" and
a bunch of the others joined in. I looked at Jono, trying
to think of how to stop him, and I was just about to open
my mouth when I noticed our visitor looking at me.

He was smiling at me so serenely that I shut my mouth
and stared. It was the most beautiful thing I have ever
seen. He glanced at Jono, who just shut up. Then he
looked back at me and I was transfixed by how beautiful
he was. There wasn't, I don't think, a visible glow around
him, but it seemed that there was because his peace and
serenity enveloped the whole room.

I don't know how long we all sat there in silence, but I eventually managed to start the class reading aloud, in turn, something that I had never been able to get them to do before. The hour passed in what seemed like five minutes. At the end of the lesson, they all left quietly and some of them even wished me a happy Easter.

I was putting my things in my bag when I noticed that the boy was standing in the doorway, the only pupil left in the room. He said, "Don't give up, miss," and then went out the door and off down the corridor. I saw Kevin Ritchie in the playground, waiting for his mum, and asked him where his cousin was, but as I think I had already realized, he said he didn't have a cousin.

I'm sure that I was visited by an angel when I desperately needed support and a bit of hope for the future. So I didn't give up; I kept on teaching and I kept the memory of his smile inside me. I wish I could tell you that the class was perfect after that, but I can't. They were much better, though—I think some of the goodness had rubbed off onto them—and whenever they acted up after that, I thought about my angel and looked at where he had sat, and it never seemed as awful ever again.

Thomas, 53
Illinois, USA

My son Tommy was kidnapped when he was only four weeks old. It was about the third or fourth time he had been out of the house. My wife took him to Wal-Mart with her. She left him in the stroller at the end of an aisle while she went to get some milk, and when she got back he was gone.

You can imagine how she was panicking. He was our first child (we have three now), and she had only taken her eyes off him for a second. She ran up and down the aisles, thinking he must still be in the store. Then she started screaming and ran out to the exit. The guard and the people working there tried to calm her down and find out what had happened, and the guard said that a woman had just gone through pushing a stroller. A few of them ran out and started searching, but it was too late; he was gone.

The police were called, and they took my wife home and tried to work out what had happened. There was CCTV in the store, and it showed a young woman walking out with the stroller. My son was clearly visible. I was called home and it was probably the worst few hours of my life. I was absolutely terrified, to the point where I could hardly breathe, let alone speak. My wife was consumed with guilt, feeling it was all her fault, and I was trying to persuade her to stay positive. But deep down, both of us were convinced we'd lost him.

Then, about midnight, a call came through on the police radio. A woman had given herself up and had handed over a baby boy she had kidnapped. Even then we couldn't be absolutely sure until we got down there and saw him for ourselves, but to our absolute relief, it was him. He was fast asleep, would you believe? He woke up for a moment because we were shouting and kissing him. He just looked confused and went back to sleep. We didn't care, because we had him back and that was all that mattered.

The woman who had brought him back was held by the police and charged. She turned out to be quite a strange girl, from way out in the country. She had split up with her husband and had had some kind of nervous breakdown. Then she decided that the way to get her husband back was to have a baby. She had been planning on telling him that it was his, and that he had to come home and help her look after it. She had been hanging around supermarkets and malls for a few days, and my wife was just incredibly unlucky to be there at the wrong time.

The woman told the police that she would have gone through with it, but while she was driving home afterward, she found an angel sitting in the passenger seat next to her. He had talked to her and explained to her why what she was doing was wrong and how upset the parents would be, and she had been unable to go through with it. So she had gone to the police and taken responsibility for her actions.

She wasn't locked up in the end; they put her in some kind of hospital and then she was kept under observation for a while. We didn't stay in touch with her, of course; we wanted nothing to do with someone who had done that to us. But I was nonetheless pleased to hear that they didn't make her suffer needlessly. It seemed like she had already been through a lot in her life, so what use would jail have been?

If it was an angel that persuaded her to change her mind, we owe that angel everything. Our whole life and marriage and family would have been completely different if we had lost Tommy. I don't know how we'd have coped. But instead, it was just a very frightening experience with a happy ending. If anything, it made us appreciate our good fortune and happiness all the more. For a long time, we found it hard to let any of our children out of our sight. But in the end we realized that you can't plan your whole life around one crazy moment.

Tommy just graduated from college last week, though he likes to be called Tom now. He's a fine young man, and of course he remembers nothing about what happened. We told him the story when he was about twelve, and he just said he was happy we got him back. Also, God bless him, he was concerned about the woman who had taken him. He said, "She must have been so sad and lonely to want a baby that much." Which I suppose is true. I can't really forgive her, but at least it all turned out for the best in the end.

CAROL, 44
Idaho, USA

I was driving to see my daughter a few years ago. She lives about a hundred miles away, so it's a fairly long drive. I was driving down the highway, down a stretch where there is a steep slope away to the right-hand side, and a rocky wall on the left-hand side.

I was feeling a little tired, but I wanted to keep going and get there before sunset. Then I heard a horn blaring behind me, and a blue car pulled alongside me. There was a man in there gesturing at me. I was angry about the horn, as I couldn't see any need for it, but he kept on pointing at my car and gesturing at me to pull over. I thought maybe there was a problem with my car, so I waved at him to say, "Okay, I'll pull over." I slowed down and pulled onto the shoulder, meaning to get out and give the car a once-over, in case he'd spotted something. He went on past and his car disappeared up around the bend.

Just as I got the car almost stopped, there was an almighty bang and the engine starting pouring out smoke. I braked hard and jumped out of the car, and then, as I got a few steps away from it, there was another bang and the engine caught fire. I ran right away from the car, and within about thirty seconds, the whole thing was on fire. It was completely wrecked. It was an extraordinary thing to have happen.

I found out later that there was a problem with that particular make of car, and that they had just started recalling them after similar fires in other cars. It would have been extremely dangerous if I had been still going at full speed when it happened. The combination of the shock and the smoke might well have meant I ended up going into the rocky wall, or rolling away down the slope. So the driver of the blue car probably saved my life. But how could he possibly have known that that was about to happen? It's not like there was any visible warning sign. To know right then that was about to happen, he must have been more than human. He must have been an angel, don't you think?

Lenie, 34
London, England

Three men tried to mug me once, and it could have been worse than that. I was walking along Caledonian Road at about 10:00 p.m. when they came up behind me and grabbed me around the neck. They were too strong for me. They dragged me into a side alley that runs along by the railway line. It is a very deserted alley; in the daytime, people use it as a short cut from the housing estate by the park, but at night most people walk the long way round to avoid cutting through such a secluded area.

They took my bag off me right away, but one of them was shouting at me, saying that they knew I had more in my pockets. One of them was holding me, while this other one started mauling me, feeling all my pockets and grabbing at me. It was extremely frightening and repulsive. At that point, there was a huge noise, a kind of shouting, and a big man stepped out through a gate in the fence to my left. He was very tall and strong looking, and he started shouting at the men to leave me alone and to drop the bag.

The nearest one to me was holding my bag and he dropped it right away. One of the others started shouting at him to pick it up, but the big man just cuffed him around the head. Then they all started to panic and ran off together up the alley. The big man told me that he was going to make sure they stayed away from me and he ran after them. It was very gratifying, after being so scared myself, to see them scared off by someone bigger.

The next day, I went to the police. I hadn't lost anything, but I thought that if those people had done that kind of thing before, it might help the police to have another witness or description. Apparently it was a gang who had been doing a lot of mugging around that area, so the police were keen to hear what I had to say. They were very nice to me about it and took down all the details. They were also very interested to try and track down the man who had rescued me. They put out those yellow crime boards you see around London, asking for more information, and asking the man who had helped me to come forward and give evidence.

He never showed up, and the one time I walked back down the alley in daylight I realized a strange thing. The gate the man had come out of didn't exist. I went over and over it in my head, and pictured where he had appeared from. It was a fence without a gate in it. No one would have put a gate there because it just leads down to the railway line. But there was nowhere else he could have come from.

The more I thought about it, the more convinced I was that something unnatural happened and that I had been rescued by someone who wasn't human. I can't see any other way to explain it. The police came back to me about six months later to follow up on the crime report, and the officer in charge told me that they hadn't had any more trouble with that particular gang. I don't know what the man did to them to stop them, but it seems he had given them a hell of a scare!

JOHNNY
Hastings, England

I saw an angel when I was a young boy. My friends and I could be naughty as lads. I remember one day we were teasing a younger boy. We didn't mean any harm, but you don't think as a youngster, do you? We were throwing bottle tops at him from across the street and a few of them hit him. He started crying and carrying on, and for a while we thought that was funny.

Then something really weird happened. In front of him this big light appeared, and an angel stood between us and the younger boy. It was huge with these great big wings. We just stood still and stared at it. I was frightened, and it was then that it dawned on us that the way we had been behaving was bad. We had been having our fun by spoiling someone else's.

We never teased anyone again, except for mild ribbing of each other and that was among friends. We never talked about what we'd seen that day. I think even if each of us saw it, no one wanted to say in case the others hadn't and thought we'd gone soft. It changed me in many ways. I began to think about other people's feelings more. I suppose you could say I grew up a bit more. I trained to be a social worker when I grew up. I wanted a job where I felt useful, like I was giving something back and atoning for my sins as a lad. Perhaps my whole life was changed by seeing that angel. I'm convinced that's what it was.

JACK, 28
Rotterdam, Holland

I believe I was saved by an angel once. It was in slightly ludicrous circumstances. I was on holiday with my parents when I was fifteen, in Lesbos in Greece at a small resort called Skala Kallonis. It was a lovely place with a very shallow bay and a small village with a few restaurants. There wasn't an awful lot to do and I got a bit bored at times, but mostly I was enjoying myself.

One afternoon my parents wanted to drive up into the hills to visit some church or monastery they'd read about in the guidebook. It seemed incredibly boring, so I managed to persuade them to let me spend the afternoon at the beach without them. They drove off with my little sister grumbling in the back seat, and left me with the room keys and enough money to get a few things.

We'd been out once or twice in pedalos—they're those little boats that you pedal like a bicycle. I'd been out with my dad and had enjoyed it, even though it's a bit of a silly way of getting from A to B. Now I decided to go out on my own. They're two-person boats, but you can pedal them by yourself. I hired one off the Greek guy on the beach, who just shrugged and sorted one out for me.

I started pedaling out, and decided to go a bit farther than I had with my dad, when we'd basically pottered up and down about twenty yards from the shore. I went quite a long way, out to where the water started to get deeper. Then I looked back at the shore, which was a fair distance away. I leaned over and started watching the fish swimming beneath the boat. All sorts of colorful fish, big and small, were flitting around down there, and I watched them for a while. Then I looked up and realized I was farther from shore than I had thought, and the breeze was getting stronger.

I started pedaling to get a little closer to shore. I pedaled and pedaled, but I didn't seem to be getting any closer. I realized that the tide was taking me away from shore faster than I could pedal back to shore. The shallow water of the bay was actually quite misleading, because it meant that the water there was very calm and the waves were tiny. But out here, the swell of the sea started to be much more noticeable and the wind was much stronger. I could see people way off on the beach, but it wasn't too far from being out of sight.

I got a bit panicky. I realized I'd come out too far and it was going to be hard work to get back. I kept trying and trying, but I was getting exhausted with the effort, and still wasn't getting any closer. In fact, I still seemed to be getting farther away. After about a quarter of an hour of this, I was really worried. It would be getting dark in another hour or two, and I really didn't want to be adrift in a stupid pedalo boat when that happened.

I actually started crying, it was so frustrating. I closed my eyes and leaned forward for a rest, all the time worrying that if I wasn't pedaling I was drifting even farther from land. Then, while my eyes were closed, I heard a voice say, "I'll help." I opened my eyes and saw nothing, but the pedals started turning of their own accord. I pushed a little to help, but they were just going round as though someone was sitting in the seat next to me doing the pedaling. It kept going and going, and all I had to do was help them round. Finally I started making some progress and getting closer to shore. After about twenty minutes, we finally got back to the shallow part, and I realized that I could keep the boat moving from there.

I said thanks, even though I couldn't see anyone. At that point, the pedals stopped going on their own and I took over. There was still a bit of water to cover, but once I was in the shallow part, I wasn't getting pushed away from land by the tide anymore. I was totally exhausted when I got back to the beach. I just went back to the room and had a shower. By the time my parents got back, I was feeling okay, even though my muscles were aching.

I didn't tell anyone at the time, since I was a teenager and easily embarrassed. But now that I'm older, I've told a few people, and it's amazing how many others have had similar experiences, or at least believe in angels enough to find it an interesting story rather than a foolish one. It's kind of funny because it happened in a pedalo, but it was still a dangerous situation, so it was good that there was someone or something there to help me out.

EDWARD
Ormston Moor, England

I was out walking on the moor with my dog Benny when a mist came down suddenly. That often happens around here; all the roads leading up to the moor have orange lights that flash, warning cars not to go up onto the moor because of the mist. This was a very heavy mist with almost nil visibility. I slipped and fell into a marsh bog, and I didn't seem to have the strength to pull myself out. They can be like that, the peat bogs. It's not like quicksand, where you might be sucked under, but it's very heavy mud and can be hard to get out of without help.

Benny ran off—I hoped to try to find help; he's a good dog, been with me for years—and eventually came back with a man. The man helped me out and walked with me in what he said was the direction of the nearest village. We chatted about this and that, and he sounded like a local man from his accent. As I got to the village, the mist had begun to clear. I turned to the man to thank him for helping me, maybe offer him a pint for his troubles. He was nowhere to be seen. I looked behind in the direction we had just come and all around, but he was gone.

People tell me I must have hallucinated him, but I'm sure he was there. My guardian angel, maybe? It would be like me to have a guardian angel that's a Yorkshire bloke who likes ale and dog racing!

Graham
Illinois, USA

I drive trucks for a living, and one of my routes out west can get very bad weather along it at certain times of year. If I haven't got a heavy load and the weather is bad, I need to wait until conditions clear up a bit or my truck could be blown over. When you're only carrying a light load, the wind can literally turn you upside down.

On this particular day, the weather seemed fairly nice and there had been no warnings on the radio, so I just set out as I usually would. However, once I got going, it seemed that the weather was turning nasty. There can be some nasty accidents along fast roads when the wind is strong. I did the usual safety drill, put on my hazard warning lights and drove as slowly and carefully as I could.

Suddenly, in front of me, another truck had stopped. The driver was standing in front of it, waving his arms for me to stop. He said that he was carrying a heavy consignment of metal and I should pull my truck over to the side and ride with him to the next town where I could arrange to get help. I didn't want to leave my truck by the side of the road, so eventually we agreed that he would go ahead and radio for help so that someone would come and rescue me. I sat in my cab and waited. After about ten minutes I fell asleep, and when I woke up, the man was beside me, driving my truck. We chatted for a while and eventually reached my destination, where I thanked him for helping me out. I took his name and number, saying maybe we could meet for a beer sometime.

I was so tired, I went to the nearby motel to sleep before going in to sign off my consignment. The next morning when I signed in, I told the staff that I had been lucky that the guy had helped me the day before. They all looked confused and asked, "What guy?" They all said that I had driven the truck in all by myself. To this day, I still can't believe that I did.

Asif, 52
Baghdad, Iraq

When the Americans came, I was pleased. I was one of those who thought that this was the only way to be rid of Saddam. But when they started bombing Baghdad, I was scared. I had no idea why they were bombing some of the places that were hit. Residential areas and schools near us got hit. You just can't be precise with bombs, I suppose, but at that point it felt as though we were under attack ourselves, not the government who were all holed up in bunkers somewhere else.

There was one particularly terrible day when there was wave after wave of attacks. Like many people, we had nowhere to hide, so we were down in the cellar praying.

There was a huge explosion nearby and the whole house shook. And then the bombs stopped. We waited another half hour or so and everything was quiet. I decided to go out onto the street to see what had happened.

A man who I knew slightly was out in the street with his family—a wife and three daughters. He lived about ten houses away from me. His house had been flattened; there was virtually nothing left except the walls of the neighbors' houses. He told me that a few minutes before the bomb hit, he had been inside the house with his family, in the cellar. He had heard someone run into the house and shout down the stairs. The voice told him to get out now, to get his family and get out of the house and across the street. Just that. He had no reason to do this, especially in the middle of an air raid. But for some reason, he trusted the voice and did as he was told.

Shortly afterward, they saw the bomb strike and the building collapse. He was in severe shock at seeing his home destroyed. But, he said, thanks to an angel, he still had his own life and the lives of his family.

POLLY, 35
South Carolina, USA

When I was ten, I nearly drowned. I was doing well at swimming in the pool, but I wasn't that strong. I was playing out there with my brother and my cousins. They were about my age, and my brother was fourteen. He was a good swimmer, and my father trusted him to look after us swimming.

I got the idea that I wanted to dive into the deep end and swim across. I'd learned how to dive with my father, so I thought I would be fine. But I hit the water too hard and hit my belly, and it took the wind out of me. I went under for a moment or two and it was hard work to get to the surface. Then I was scared and panting hard, and I started trying to scramble toward the side, but I just didn't have the strength. I think it was because I was panicking and hyperventilating, and that just took all my energy away.

I felt heavier and heavier and I started to go under. I tried to shout, but I just got water in my mouth. Everyone else was horsing around with a ball down at the other end of the pool, and I didn't think they could see the trouble I was in. I took a big mouthful of air and tried to get going, but I just started to sink. I remember very clearly looking up from under the water. I could see my cousins at the other end, and I could see the sun shining very clearly in the sky. It seemed like a terrible way to die, in broad daylight, with people all around.

I was holding my breath and trying to kick, but it wasn't making any difference. The light started to go dark above me. Then all at once I felt hands holding me up and pushing me upward, and at the same time I heard a splash. There were hands all around me, all pushing upward. I had to breathe and opened my mouth, and just water came in, a terrible feeling. But still the hands were pushing and dragging me, and I thought that somehow all my cousins must be there, helping my brother. Or perhaps my parents had come out. Gradually I was hauled to the surface and over the edge, and then I just about passed out. I felt people pushing me around and banging at me, and then I don't remember anything until I woke up on the sofa later, feeling like I'd swallowed something nasty, with my chest hurting like hell.

Afterward I found out what had happened. My brother had seen me in trouble. He had told the cousins to run and find my parents, because they were too little to help. Then he had climbed out of the other end of the pool and run down to jump in beside me. He had managed to get hold of my arms and drag me to the surface. He had held me there for a moment or two, unable to get me out and scared that I was dying, when my father ran out of the house and pulled me out. My father had pumped at my chest to get the water out and given me artificial respiration, but that must have been after I'd passed out.

Now that all makes sense, except that I know there was more than one person in the water. There were hands holding me up before my brother got there to drag me up. And even as he was pulling, I could feel them pushing me. I asked my brother about it recently. I've never stopped thanking him for saving me, but I asked him if he was absolutely sure no one else helped. He said it was strange that I asked, because he had tried to pull me, and had felt I was too heavy and that it was hopeless. Then he said that I just seemed to rise out of the water as though I was being pushed. So how I remember it is backed up by what he told me. Someone helped. He saved me, but he might not have been able to do it alone, so he got some help when he needed it.

JACK, 43
Illinois, USA

An angel once stopped me from making a terrible mistake. I used to work for a media company. I had a desk job, which was interesting, but quite a few of my colleagues traveled around the world, selling and presenting our products. At the time my wife was not especially well, but we were trying for a baby anyway.

I went in one day and found out that the colleague who shared an office with me was leaving the company. He had a traveling job, and my boss called me into his office and offered me the job. It was considerably better paid than the job I was doing, and his assumption was that I would say yes. However, I hesitated and asked for time to think about it.

I knew my wife wouldn't be pleased. She had said several times that she didn't understand how my colleagues coped with the travel, and that she felt sorry for their wives. It was clear that she would not think it was good news. But on the other hand, we really needed the extra money if we were going to have a baby, and I had the very strong feeling that turning the job down would label me as unambitious and would be a black mark against me at work. The pressure that this kind of situation creates is hard to explain. A lot of it is self-imposed, but there is a genuine concern that the people at work who already

live their lives in that very difficult way would find it fee-
ble if you refused to do the same. They might even take it
as an unspoken criticism of the way they choose to live.
The assumption is that you should do what the company
needs you to do, and your family should live with it.

Rather than talk to my wife about it, I just went back
that afternoon and accepted the job. I suppose I thought
I could explain to her why I felt I had to do it. But when
I got home and told her, she was furious. She was asking
how we could cope with a child if I was away every other
month. I was telling her that her mother and sisters could
help, and my family. But she said she didn't want their
help; she wanted me at home. Then I got angry because I
felt she didn't understand the stress I was under.

We shouted a lot of stupid things we didn't mean and
went to bed without making up. I slept in the spare room
by myself. I had a funny dream, where I was playing chess
with an angel. We were in a grand, empty, wood-pan-
eled room somewhere. It looked like a gentlemen's club
or library. He was a really proper angel with wings and a
halo and everything. We were talking about all sorts of
things: baseball, world politics, my job and my family—it
was like having a beer with a friend. I can't remember
all of what we said, but that's how I remember it. But he
kept coming back to one point: why I had taken the job.
He was saying that what I had to work out was whether I
had done it for my wife and child, or for me. And I kept
saying I didn't have a child yet, but he said it didn't matter. Was it for me or for my wife and child? It was like

a close friend who is such a good friend that he can say the things you don't want to hear. We finished the chess game (I lost, of course) and then I woke up.

I spent the morning thinking about everything I had dreamed about. Today I don't care if that was a real angel or not, because either way, he told me things I needed to hear. But that morning I had just had the dream and I firmly believed it was a real angel who had come to give me a message. I went in to my boss and told him I wasn't taking the job after all. All hell broke loose, and they tried to bully and threaten me into taking it. That actually made me feel less guilty. If they hadn't reacted so badly, I might have felt I was letting them down. But actually they just showed me how little they cared about me personally, so why should I care about them? The thing about that kind of pressure is that as long as you give in to it, it's still there, but once you're brave enough to resist it, you realize that there is nothing they can do to you after all.

The thing is, I had realized that the angel was right. I had only been taking the job for myself. I had secretly wanted to travel and been jealous of my colleagues who did. It seemed more fun than what I did. But I had dressed all this up in my mind as being about more than that; I had wanted to believe I was doing the right thing by trying to get ahead at work and make more money. But that wasn't really why I was doing it. And as soon as I realized that, I had the courage to change my mind.

Also, the fact that the angel kept referring to my
child made me put myself in the position of parent for
the first time. I had thought about having children, but I
just imagined playing with them, and taking them out in
the stroller to show them the park and the animals and
things like that. Now for the first time I felt that weight
of responsibility that only parents truly know. I thought
about how I'd feel if I really had a child, and I realized
that I couldn't take the job if I couldn't swear I'd want
it if I really had a child. So once I really thought about
what it meant to my wife and imaginary child, I saw that
being selfish wasn't the right thing to do.

After I had told my boss, I went back to my office and
my wife called. I hadn't talked to her since our argument
the night before. She was still very agitated and sounded
stressed. But right away I told her that I realized she was
right and I had turned the job down. Then she was very
relieved. She told me later that she had been calling to
tell me she was leaving me and going back to her mother,
because she was so upset that I had done this without
consulting her. But the fact that I had belatedly realized
that I was in the wrong made up for it a bit.

The other strange thing about all this is that a week
later, I got another phone call from my wife. She had just
done a test and found out that she was pregnant. I was so
happy I just walked out on work for the day and bought
some flowers and went home to her. She told me she had
been wondering, but had woken up that day feeling sick
and had gotten the test. But for it to show up positive,

she must have actually been pregnant already the week before, when I dreamed about the angel. So perhaps that was why the angel kept referring to my child. It might also explain why the angel thought it was important enough to talk to me. He might even have cared more about the child than about me, which would be fair because that's how I feel now. Imagine what a mess we would have been in if I'd been pig-headed and kept the job, and my wife had gone home to her mother. Maybe we could have figured it out, but maybe it would have been too much of a mess.

The other thing I should mention is that, while the atmosphere at work was strained for a while, I ended up enjoying my job more since I was no longer wanting to travel, and the individuals who had made my life difficult for not traveling ended up leaving the company anyway. In the end, it didn't matter or do me any harm. In fact, I think it did me good, because it showed me that you can stand up for yourself and do the right thing for your family in the face of intimidation. So all around, the fact that I stayed and figured it out was the best possible thing for us. I've got three children now and I simply can't imagine life without them.

Moira
Aylesbury, England

My husband was attacked by a gang of youths once. We live in a neighborhood that is quite rough, and the gangs had been getting worse and worse. They would hang around the shops, start fires in the bins, spray obscene graffiti, and generally make everyone's lives a misery. One night they had been doing all their usual stuff when Martin looked out the window and saw them messing about with his car. They had a coat hanger and they were obviously trying to break into it. Right there outside our house in broad daylight.

I wish I'd been there, because I would have told him to leave them alone, or at least to call the police. But he just went out and started shouting at them. Instead of stopping what they were doing, they turned on him and started hitting and kicking him. He got a kick in the head that knocked him out and still they didn't stop.

I got a call at work from my neighbors. They said Martin was being taken in an ambulance. Of course I went to the hospital and he was a right mess. He was unconscious all night and the doctors were getting me ready for the idea he might die. But he hung in there and made it through. I didn't leave the hospital for three days, until I was absolutely sure he was okay. But the police came and talked to me.

Everyone knew who the kids were, of course, but the problem was getting people to talk about it in court. Luckily there were enough of my neighbors who were brave enough to identify the kids. I talked to the neighbor who had called me, and he told me that he had looked out because there had been a flash of light, which seemed strange, and then he had seen my husband lying there and the kids running away. But he recognized them, even so, and he was one of those who testified against them. It was a risky thing because their families were rough, but in the end all they did was threaten people and shout a lot. No one got hurt, except of course my husband who was still in the hospital recovering.

There was a court hearing that lasted a few days, as they wouldn't plead guilty. There were six of them. Most of them were nasty pieces of work, sneering and swaggering, and thinking they could just deny everything and lie their way out of trouble. They got put away for a year or so each, because they all had previous records. Not long enough, but it was apparently the most we could expect.

The last one was different. He seemed a bit backward, and he talked about the whole thing as if he was a little kid being led around playing games or something. He was the brother of one of the worst of them, so I suppose in a way that's what he was. He said a very strange thing in his evidence. He said they were there fighting—that's what he called it, even though there were six of them and only one of Martin. But then he said that there had been a loud bang, and three tall men were suddenly there chasing them away. He sounded terrified, and at that point all the others looked a bit strange, as though they didn't want to admit they had been scared too. No one else saw anyone there at all. Some people from down the road specifically said that they had seen the six hitting Martin, then running away, no one else in sight.

I can't get it out of my head that Martin might have been rescued by angels. He got hurt badly enough, in any case. His ankle was smashed and he couldn't work for six months, and he still gets headaches. But he's basically okay. The kids got out of prison, of course, but at least three of them are back inside already. I don't know or care what happened to the others, but I heard that the sixth one, who had talked about the angels, was put into some kind of medical care rather than into prison. I thought that was probably fair. He didn't seem to be evil, just manipulated, or badly influenced by his brother and so-called friends. Martin's back at work now, and the area has improved a bit since that those particular kids aren't here any more. But we're about to move away, because there are bad memories here for us now.

CHARLIE, 36
New York, USA

I went hiking on my own in the Appalachians when I was twenty-two. It was a kind of rite of passage for me to go up into the wild and be by myself for a while. I was well prepared; I've been out in the wilderness plenty of times with my father and uncle. But I wanted to do it alone.

One thing that always does worry me out there in the woods is bears. I know what to do in theory, but I worry about whether I'll remember it all in the moment of actually meeting a bear—will I remember which one to run from and which one to play dead for, will I be able to run or climb fast enough, and so on. I met a smallish bear once with my father, but he just stared at us down the path and ambled away so we didn't need to do a thing.

The only other time I met a bear was on this solo trip. It was about two in the morning and I was lying in my tent in the dark. It was a beautiful clear night. The stars were so clear up in the sky and there wasn't a sound of people or cars anywhere, just the sounds of the woods. Then I heard the bear. I'd tied all my food up in the tree so I thought it would ignore me, but instead it came closer. I could hear it grunting and walking around. I think it was looking for something to eat. I was pretty scared in the tent. It didn't seem like a good idea to come out and confront it, so I lay as still as possible, trying to breathe very quietly, and hoping it would go away. I could hear all these strange little noises it was making, and then suddenly there was a scraping sound, and the tent was moving. The bear was trying to get into the tent, or at least it was pawing at the tent to see what happened.

It was frightening, and I really wasn't sure what to do. Then I heard a voice outside. It was a very quiet, serene voice, almost whispering. It said something like, "Come on over here, you silly bear." And then it kept saying "Come on," over and over. The bear stopped pawing at my tent and I could hear it start to move away. For a while I was too scared to move, but as the sound moved farther and farther away, my curiosity overcame me. Who on earth would come up there in the middle of the night just to lead a bear away from my tent?

I unzipped the tent and leaned out around the corner, and by the moonlight I could just see the shape of a man walking off into the woods. There was a big bear, one of the biggest I've seen, ambling gently after the man. You could see the bear wasn't chasing the man, just following him. I watched them for a few moments, and then they were out of sight.

After that I was awake pretty much all night. But I didn't feel scared, just amazed by what I had seen. The next day, I continued walking, all the way up to the end of the trail. I went on being as cautious as ever. After all, I may have been lucky, or had some help that time, but that's no reason to stop taking the basic precautions, is it?

MIKE, 28
Wrexham, Wales

When I was about ten years old, I went on holiday with my parents to Fuerteventura in the Canary Islands. I was very excited in the car on the way to the airport because I'd never been on a plane before. I don't actually recall much about the flight, but I do remember how hot it was when we got off the plane at the other end. It felt like we were stepping into a big cushion of warmth—especially as it had been snowing back in England.

The place where we were staying was next to a small beach set in a cove with a long pier on the left, which had a white lighthouse standing at the very end. The other side was covered with lines of small apartments that reached out to the tip of the land. I used to sit in the surf in a rubber ring that my dad had bought me at one of the tourist shops and spin myself around so that the lighthouse and the villas blurred together.

There wasn't much to do apart from play on the beach and swim while my mum and dad lay in the sun, but I didn't get bored. There were a few other kids that I messed around with sometimes, but mostly I amused myself by trying to copy the sand sculptures that an aging hippie used to build up next to the seawall where everybody got down onto the beach. He had a blue plastic sandwich box next to his creations that he'd throw a handful of loose change into, hoping that impressionable kids like me would add to it.

The third or fourth day we were there, I can't remember exactly, he'd made a life-sized dolphin. I spent most of the morning trying to do the same down near the sea but, no matter how hard I tried or however many times I kicked it to pieces and started again, I just couldn't get it right. I ended up covered in sand that stuck to me all over and was beginning to make me scratchy and irritable, so I ran down to the sea and dived into an incoming wave. I was a pretty strong swimmer for my age—I'd learned at the local pool, when I was eight, with my dad—and I got about twenty yards from the beach in a minute or so.

The trouble was that the water was still quite shallow for about fifty yards and it was almost lukewarm from the heat of the sun. I knew from experience that it cooled down dramatically after that, and I wanted to cool off and get every bit of sand off my skin, so I kept going. Once I got into the colder water, I played around for a bit, dunking my head underwater and trying to catch some of the little fish that darted about just under the surface. I must have drifted a bit farther than I thought, because when I tried to put my feet down, I couldn't feel the bottom. I looked back toward the beach and I realized that I'd gotten myself about a hundred yards out—much farther than I'd ever been before. That scared me a bit, but I knew I wouldn't have any trouble doing the distance, so I started swimming back to the shore.

What I hadn't realized was that the tide was on its way out, as it had been when I'd first got into the water—the reason I'd gotten so far out. Swimming back was much harder going and I didn't really seem to be getting anywhere. Even after five minutes, the beach looked just as far away as it had been when I'd originally turned back. If anything, I seemed to be going backward. After getting slapped in the face by a couple of waves, I really got frightened.

My arms were getting tired and I'd lost all the rhythm of my swimming when I suddenly became aware of a firm pressure on my belly and chest. It felt exactly like my dad's hands had felt when he was teaching me to swim and holding me up in the water, so much so that I actually shouted out, "It's okay, Dad, I'm doing it!" just like I used to when I'd nearly got it.

At the same time I heard a voice just above me say, "You're doing great, Mike. Just try and go with the swell." I knew it wasn't my dad, because he was asleep on the beach, but I instantly forgot about being scared because I realized I was going to be safe. The hands kept on holding me on the surface and helping me forward through the water. I started judging the swell of the waves, just like the voice had said, and the beach got closer and closer.

When I was nearly there I felt the hands disappear. I panicked and kicked downward, but I was back in my depth and my feet touched the bottom. I stood up and looked back out to where I'd been, but there was no one there. I knew I hadn't imagined that voice or the secure pressure of hands on my body. I truly believed then, and I believe now, that an angel saved my life that day. I like to think that even now, if I got out of my depth, he'd look out for me again.

CAROL, 54
Singapore

I met an angel fifteen years ago when I was going through a very difficult time in my life. I had gotten badly in debt while traveling and working abroad, and I'd had to move back in with my parents, in Sussex in England. I was working at the dentist in this little town where I had grown up, as a receptionist. My parents weren't very sympathetic, the job was boring, and it just felt like I'd been defeated.

I got quite depressed and started sleeping in late at the weekends, staying in bed all day watching television. I justified it by saying that I was trying to avoid spending money to get out of debt faster, but then I'd go on these shopping sprees where I bought clothes I didn't really need to make myself feel better. Of course, then I just felt guilty and depressed all over again.

One Sunday morning after I'd done exactly that, I woke up really early. I would normally have rolled over and gone back to bed until midday, but instead I opened my eyes and looked around, and the room was full of a really strange light. It felt warm, like the brightest sunlight you've ever seen. And then that faded, and there was just the street-light coming through the curtains, but it had given me a strange, restless feeling, so I got up and got dressed.

I got in my little car and set off without knowing where I was going. Then I knew that I had to go to Ditchling Beacon, which is the highest hill in the South Downs. You can drive right up to the top and then walk along a footpath looking down on the countryside. I went up there and got out, and it was just dawn. I set off down the path and walked and walked, not really thinking. Then I looked around and saw there was a boy walking beside me. I didn't know where he'd come from. He was about twenty, with a pale face and a serious expression.

We started talking. He asked me why I was there and I told him everything. It seemed natural for some reason, in this unnatural situation. I asked him why he was there, but he just smiled and avoided the question and kept talking about me. I wasn't scared of him, but it did seem very strange to me even at the time. I told him all about why I wasn't happy and how stuck I felt. It was kind of like a therapy session, but he seemed very wise and old for his years. He told me that being stuck was something that was in my head, and that the feeling of being defeated was something I'd imposed on myself out of shame. He said I had to forget the shame, forget what other people thought, and look at what was best for me. He also said that because of how I was feeling, I was making other people unhappy, like my parents. I had told him a little about them, but what he said made it sound as if he already knew about it all, better than me.

He said that doing what was best for me wasn't selfish, it was the most considerate thing I could do, because if I could be happy, I'd make others happy too. It was lovely talking to him, because I could feel all these silly attitudes I'd built up to protect myself falling away, and the real me was still there, even if it had been a while since I'd seen her.

After a little while we'd said everything that needed to be said, but I kept walking and thinking, and he was walking beside me. Then I turned to ask him again about himself, and he was gone, just like that. I walked back to the car, feeling quite strange and excited. I quit my job the next day, and a week after that I set off to London to find a new job. I was pretty lucky, because I managed to find a job working over the summer in a holiday resort in the Mediterranean. It wasn't such a great job, but it was a start, and most importantly, it got me moving again after such a passive time in my life.

It was a struggle to get out of debt, but I worked at it in a more positive way, rather than getting depressed, and eventually I got myself a better job too, which helped. I never looked back, and here I am now on the other side of the world, happy in what I'm doing here. I probably get along better with my parents than when I lived with them, as well, so all around it was the right thing to do. But I needed to regain enough positivity even to take the first step, so I'm glad I met the angel that morning and listened to what he told me.

KARL-HEINZ, 55
Munich, Germany

I am a train driver. I've never been involved in a real accident, thankfully, but the one time I had a close miss makes quite an interesting story. I was coming around a long curve that runs alongside the woods at the edge of the city. There are often children playing beside the tracks there, because there are paths through from the woods. I'm always concerned to see them there unsupervised, but nothing had ever happened.

This time, it seemed that they were playing some kind of game of dare, which involved running on to the tracks and then off again. I've seen this sort of thing a few times, and it makes me very angry. It is very stressful for the driver to be put in that position. I braked a little for safety. They seemed to be getting clear in plenty of time. But then the last boy—he looked to be no more than about ten years old—he slipped or got his foot stuck, and fell. I was only about a hundred meters away at this point and I applied the brakes fully, hoping to give him a little time. His friends had run away a short distance after they left the tracks, and only turned round to see him lying there after it was too late to run back and help.

He was struggling to get to his feet. I remember all this very clearly. It's like a piece of slow-motion film that has been imprinted on my brain, because I was so scared that I was about to be responsible for killing this boy. It was simply impossible to stop in the distance available.

Then I saw a man run onto the tracks from the left-hand side, very fast. He was in a black suit and middle-aged, but I couldn't see his face. He grabbed the boy's arm and hauled him off the tracks with only seconds to spare. I don't think the boy would have made it otherwise.

I screeched to a halt, about a hundred meters too late. I was talking over the radio to the guard, farther back down the train, telling him that a boy had nearly been hit. As soon as the train stopped, he jumped off and ran after the children. We take safety very seriously, and it is important to try and catch these people if possible, if only to make it clear to them how serious their behavior is.

The boy who had fallen had actually twisted his ankle quite badly and was limping. Most of the boys had run away, but one had the decency to stay behind and look after his friend. Because of this, the guard was able to catch them both. By the time I got out and ran back, I found him there shouting at them for being so stupid, saying didn't they know they could have been killed.

They were very shame-faced, and perhaps because one was hurt (and had nearly died) and the other was honest enough to take the blame and brave enough to stay behind with his friend, we didn't give them as hard a time as we might. They were white as sheets, anyway, and had probably learned their lesson.

I asked them where the man had gone. They didn't know what I was talking about. The one who had stayed hadn't seen any man, even though he had been looking straight at his friend as the train came toward him. The one from the tracks seemed a little confused, but his friend was very clear that he had got clear by himself. It was interesting, though, that he first said that his friend had been thrown clear, then corrected himself and said that he had somehow managed to jump. It was as though he had seen him be picked up and thrown by an invisible force, but couldn't rationalize it in his mind and so had decided that he must have jumped.

We let them go with a stern lecture. I was very relieved not to have killed the boy. I have met men who were driving a train when someone committed suicide by jumping in front of it, and no matter how much they know that they aren't truly responsible, it is clearly a heavy burden and one that often gives them nightmares and fears about driving again. If it was an angel who saved the boy, he did both of us a big favor.

ABRAHAM, 68
Maine, USA

We live in an area of very steep hills. One day my wife had a dream where an angel came to her and told her I shouldn't drive the truck the next day. She begged me not to drive, but I had to go to collect some pallets of wood, so I wanted to ignore her. I thought she was just being irrational—if we lived our lives by following every superstitious fear, where would we be? But she was so adamant, I decided to postpone the trip until another day. The route I had to take was one that went along some steep mountain roads and valleys.

Next day, I did take the truck out, but only to go to the village to pick up a few things from the store. When I reached the edge of the village, I tried to brake and found that there was no power in the brakes at all. I tried to control the truck and managed to get it into a bit of a skid across the road. It was stopped by running into a large tree that was growing by the sidewalk. The tree was damaged by the collision (which didn't make anyone very happy, as it was a lovely old tree), and my truck got a bad dent in the side, but I wasn't hurt, just a bit shaken.

It turned out that the brakes were completely gone. Lord knows what might have happened to me if I'd gone across the mountains with it in that state. I would quite possibly have been dead rather than just shaken up. These days I tend to listen to my wife's dreams and superstitions a little bit more than I used to.

BELLA, 35
Rome, Italy

I used to get bullied at school. It's a horrible thing to be bullied. A lot of it was not about physical violence, but about being ganged up on by the other girls. They would be snickering at me as I went by and I wouldn't know why. Or my bag would be pushed on the floor, and while I was leaning down to get it, my work would be scribbled on. And because no one wanted to be left out of the gang, no one would help me.

One day it got so bad I walked out of school. I had talked to the teachers and no one would do anything. My parents just used to tell me to be strong, but that wasn't enough. I felt really desperate and wanted to just run away or to die. I was walking down a road leading out of town when a woman walked up to me and asked me if I wanted a cup of coffee. It was an odd start, but she turned out to be a great help to me. She took me to a cafe and bought me coffee. And then she started to ask me about who I was and what I was doing. I told her everything.

I don't have any real reason to tell you that this woman was an angel. It is just a feeling I have, because of the way she came from nowhere and tried to help me. I can't explain it any other way than that she was there to help me and look after me. What she did was to talk to me a lot about how I felt, and also she tried to explain to me that just because everyone was joining in the bullying didn't mean they all wanted to do it. She told me that often girls join in this sort of thing because they don't want to be the only one not to. She told me to look around next time and see if I thought that there were some girls who really didn't like what they saw. She also told me that my parents were trying not to hear anything bad, because if something was wrong in my life, they blamed themselves.

This all seems quite obvious now that I am grown up, but to a fourteen-year-old girl this was all quite a revelation. The things she said gave me a real incentive to go back and try again. And she was right. I tried talking to my parents differently. I tried explaining that it was nothing to do with anything they had or hadn't done for me, but that there was this situation at school that made life difficult. After that, they were much more willing to help. They came into school with me and talked to the teachers, and as a result the teachers started paying more attention and sometimes preventing the problems from developing. Other times, I did as the woman had suggested and looked around at the group of girls. I soon realized that the real problem was the two or three girls who always led the trouble. And I even started feeling a little sorry for them in a weird way, because I realized how twisted they must be if that was all they could do to impress people.

Gradually things improved. I was lucky in that I never got hurt too badly and came out the other side without too much trouble. But bullying among children is a terrible thing and something all parents should watch out for. I was lucky that I was helped at a crucial moment, and that it made things better.

ALAN, 43
Illinois, USA

After my wife left me, I spent most of my time drinking. I was really depressed and I used that as an excuse. But really I was turning into an alcoholic. I would wake up with a hangover, have a few drinks at lunchtime to get over it, and then drink all evening. At home, I would drink a six-pack of beer, then move on to the whiskey while I was sitting there watching television. I was letting myself fall apart and blaming my wife for going. But the truth is she had good reason for going. I was already drinking too much before she left and that was one of her problems with me.

I managed to hang on to my job somehow, even though I was often a bit drunk in the afternoons. But one Friday my boss gave me a formal warning for being late and for not getting all my work done. I was in real danger of losing the job and going into a total decline.

I drank all weekend and had a terrible hangover on Monday. I called in sick and started drinking again, just sitting there in the kitchen. I think, left to my own devices, I would have sat there all week until they called me to tell me not to bother coming back. After a few hours, I felt sleepy and I leaned forward onto the table. Then there was a rattle at the door and this man came in. I had no idea how he had gotten into the house or who he was. I asked him something, but he just shook his head at me.

He took the bottle of whiskey off the table and started pouring it down the drain. I shouted at him, but he gave me such a stern glare I just sat back down. Then he went around the whole house and got every bit of alcohol he could find and poured every drop down that drain. There was a whole pile of empty bottles. Then he left. I just sat there feeling bewildered and empty.

I went to bed and fell asleep, and woke up at about six the next morning. I had a hangover, but it wasn't too bad because I had slept so long. I went into work and the first thing I did was go talk to my boss and promise him that he was going to see an improvement. From that day, I stopped drinking completely for years. I have the odd glass or two now that I've got my life back together, but I remember clearly how close I was to throwing everything away, and I never get drunk anymore.

CAROLINE, 38
Hong Kong, China

My husband got a job in Hong Kong when I was thirty. It was for a minimum of two years. It was very well paid, and we felt like it would be a mistake to turn it down. I gave up the job I had at the time at a local solicitor's office, and we both moved there. We didn't have children, so it seemed like an opportunity for some adventure. But to start with I hated it. My husband worked long hours and we lived on the thirtieth floor of a high-rise apartment block. I hated the lifts but the stairs were impossible. I didn't know anyone, and there didn't seem to be any way of meeting anyone other than my husband's colleagues, who I didn't really like.

Because I had no friends, I was spending more and more time in the flat, watching incomprehensible television programs and getting more and more depressed. I started to resent my husband and to feel like he had forced me to give up everything to be here. In fact, it had been a decision we made together, but at that stage he was all right because he was busy all the time. I was the one who was miserable.

One day I had a panic attack in the lift. I stopped it ten floors below our apartment and got out. I stayed there for a while, trying to get my breath back, and just to calm down. I was frustrated because I felt like I was becoming more and more helpless. At home I had been a competent, organized person. Here I was just a silly, scared girl.

I started to walk up the stairs to my apartment. A couple of floors below our apartment, a woman of about my age walked out from the hallway and started walking behind me. She asked if I'd walked all the way, and I told her that I'd gotten scared in the lift and had walked ten floors. She laughed, but in a nice way, and asked if I wanted to have a coffee and tell her more.

She said was called Kim Smith, and it seemed that she was in a similar position to me. She said that she too was a little bit lost here and her husband was out all the time. So she came in for coffee and soon we were talking about everything. She stayed a few hours that day and we arranged to meet again.

We became great friends and started to go out and explore a bit more. I realized that I'd been missing out by not getting out and about much. The city is an amazing place, even if it is a bit intimidating at times. Kim took me to some nice shops, cafés, and galleries, and in one English café there was a notice board with some adverts. I joined a book group and started to make more friends.

After a month or so of this, I started to see less of Kim. Not because we were less good friends, but because I was busier and she came round less often. I never went to her apartment; she always came to mine. I was happier because I was starting to settle in and I had gotten over my anxieties. One day I realized I hadn't seen her for two weeks, so I went looking for her. I asked the concierge where she lived but he couldn't tell me. There wasn't a family of that name living in the block, especially not two floors down where she had said she lived. I knocked on every door on that floor and she wasn't there. No one had recently moved in or out, either. I was quite worried and a bit disconcerted. Then I got a postcard from her. It was just a funny picture of some children with a little note saying that she was sorry not to have said goodbye, but she hoped that everything was working out for me now, wishing me all the best, and saying she was sure we'd meet again sometime.

I think back on her with great fondness, as she made the transition to that new life so much easier. I ended up having a good couple of years, but it could have been much worse. It seems like a mundane thing for an angel to help with, but I can't help wondering if she was more than just a friend. The way she disappeared was very strange, and it seemed odd that she was there at exactly the moment I needed her most and then left once the problem was solved. Also, when I try to picture her face, I have a strange sensation. I just see this smile and a kind of light, but it's hard to pin down exactly what she looked like. It's very strange and perhaps I'll never really know, but whoever she was, she was a great help to me in a difficult time.

HELEN
The Cotswolds, England

I've seen angels three times in my life, and each time it has been a totally different experience. You asked me about what angels look like, but I don't think I can really tell you.

The first time was when I was giving birth to my first child. I had to have an emergency caesarean and so I was there on an operating table, with a curtain hiding the lower half of my body, on a local anesthetic. It is a very strange thing, to feel that they are pulling and cutting down there but not to feel pain. There were quite a few people in the room. Several doctors, an anesthetist, some nurses, and my husband. He wasn't being much use, as he was feeling pretty queasy, but he was doing his best to help anyway, poor thing.

There was also someone else there, a woman who looked quite different from everyone else. She wasn't in surgical gear and she clearly wasn't quite real. She was standing behind the nurse beside me, smiling down at me.

But she was also transparent; I could see the wall behind her. I was a bit confused but I knew that she was there to look after me. I could tell that no one else could see her. When the baby was born, before they showed it to me, they took it to the table to check it over, and I could tell they were worried for a moment because they seemed to have trouble getting it to breathe. They were very tense and my husband looked worried, but the angel just stood there and smiled at me and I knew it was okay. Then the baby started crying and they all relaxed and brought her over. She had to go into emergency care for observation and the angel went away with her, so I knew she was in good hands.

The second time I met angels was when my third child, a daughter, was three. After eight years as a housewife and mother, I was going through a difficult time. I felt like no one ever cared about me or noticed me. It's like you become invisible. My husband would come home from work and pick up one of the girls and start playing with her and throwing her around. But he wouldn't come and hug me or talk to me. I had become very depressed and couldn't think of a way out. This particular day, everything had gone wrong from the start. The baby had broken my favorite vase when she was throwing her ball, she had spilled all her food, and then the washing machine broke and water went everywhere, all over the kitchen and hall, so I had to mop all that up.

Finally, at about four in the afternoon, I couldn't take any more. Annie fell asleep in her room for a nap. I poured some milk and left it for when she woke up, then called my husband's secretary and left a message that he was to come home as soon as he could. Then I just walked out. The elder children were due to be picked up by a friend that day from school, so they would be all right.

I started walking up the road with a little bag of clothes. I was running away from home, and I had no idea where I was going, except that I couldn't stay. It sounds terrible to walk out on your children like that, but sometimes it is so hard.

A man in a car stopped and offered me a lift. He didn't even ask where I was going, and because I didn't care, I just said yes, thinking I'd get as far away as I could. But he started talking to me and asking what I was doing. He had a very trustworthy face, and for some reason I found myself telling him everything. He was sympathetic, but asked me about how the children would feel and how my husband would cope. Then he suggested that I tell my husband more about what I needed. I wasn't sure that would work, but we talked about it all, and the more I talked the more ridiculous it seemed to just run away.

I asked him to turn around and take me home, but it seemed he had just been driving in circles anyway, and we were already right at the end of my road. He took me back, and when we got to the house, the front door was open and there was a woman inside. The man told me she had been looking after Annie but didn't explain any more than that. Then they both went away, leaving me to think of a sensible story to tell my husband when he got home from work. I was so relieved to see Annie was okay and so full of guilt that I had tried to leave.

That time the angels helped me in a very specific way and they just looked like ordinary people. There was no magical way of fixing things with my husband but we both tried to make things better, and I learned not to bottle things up, so that I didn't get to that state again without letting him know when I was unhappy. And we've managed to get through and enjoy life overall.

The last time I saw angels was entirely different. There was a man who shot a lot of children dead at a school in Hungerford. It didn't directly affect me, but it was all over the news and my children were the same age as some of those who died. For whatever reason, it had an enormous emotional effect on me, and I found myself crying about it a lot, in between feeling blessed that my children and my family had never suffered that way.

I don't go to church much, but I am a believer in my own way, and I went to church on a Thursday, to a morning service. I sat there in the church, not really listening to what was going on, but praying inside and listening to the songs and the organ. And when I looked up, I saw that there were angels all around us in that church. You couldn't see their faces but there were bright, shining figures everywhere I looked. I was really happy to see them, as I felt that they were there to support and protect us. I could see them for quite a long time, and then when I couldn't see them anymore, it didn't matter because I knew they were still there.

So you see, each time was quite different, but each time it was at a critical moment in my life. And in between I have always known that they were there, even when I couldn't actually see them.

JIM
Adelaide, Australia

I had been digging in the garden at the back of my house when I suddenly started to feel a bit strange. I had a crushing pain in my left arm and my chest felt constricted so I couldn't breathe properly. My house is at the end of a long road, quite away from any neighbors' houses, and my wife had gone over to see her mother, so there was no one home. I remember thinking, "I'm having a heart attack," and I tried to get to the house to phone an ambulance. I didn't manage to get far because the pain became excruciating and I collapsed on the grass.

I vaguely remember a man standing next to my garden fence, telling me that it was all right and that someone was coming for me. The next thing I knew, my wife was with me and had called an ambulance. She told me that she came as quickly as she could after the doctor had telephoned her to tell her to come home as soon as possible. It was only later as I recovered in hospital that I thought—hold on, there was no doctor, and I never gave anyone her mother's number. I think the man by the fence must have been some sort of angel.

ELIZABETH
The Cotswolds, England

My cottage is quite far away from any others on the far edge of my village. One summer day a few years ago, I was gardening, something I've always loved doing. I have won prizes for my garden. Suddenly I got a severe pain in my head that became worse. I felt dizzy and my eyesight went, turning everything gray. I think I fell to the ground.

I remember being helped by a very kind woman who called an ambulance and got me to the hospital. Apparently I had had a stroke. When I regained consciousness in the hospital, the woman was sitting beside my bed, holding my hand. She smiled at me and I felt calm and fell back to sleep. I was still very tired. Next time I awoke, the woman had gone. I asked the nurses if they had gotten the name of my visitor because I wanted to thank her. The nurses said I had had no visitors since being admitted. My daughter tells me I must have been dreaming, but I never found out who saved me. A woman had called an ambulance to my address, but the hospital workers say I was alone in the garden when they arrived. She must have been some kind of angel. It's comforting to know you're being looked after.

PASCAL, 45
Montreal, Canada

I have a problem with my eyesight that goes back to something that happened when I was twenty. I got beaten up very badly by a gang. It was ironic, because I intervened to save someone who was being robbed on the street. He was being mugged by two guys with knives, and I went up and told them that the police had been called and told them to get lost.

But then they followed me, and I unfortunately went down into this underground car park. It was quite late at night and there were three of them. I was a big, strong guy at twenty, but even so there was nothing I could do. So I got hit and kicked a lot, and ended up on the floor with my hand over my face, almost unconscious. I had a couple of broken ribs, a lot of bruising, and worst of all, a fractured skull from a kick in the face.

They left me there and it was a desolate place—no guarantee that anyone would find me, and I was in a bad way. I couldn't see too well; I had blood in one eye and I guess I was concussed. I started trying to struggle to my feet so I could go get help. But then there was a voice talking to me. It was saying, "It's okay, someone's coming. Don't move. Someone's coming." This went on for quite a while, perhaps a quarter of an hour, though it was hard to tell. I thought that meant that help had been called. I couldn't see the person talking or even tell if it was a man or a woman, but they were definitely sitting next to me on the ground. And then I heard someone else, someone different, shout, "Oh God! What happened? Are you all right?" There were two of them, so one ran to a telephone while the other stayed with me.

At the hospital, the doctor told me I could have made my fractured skull a lot worse by getting up and blundering around. As it was, my eye was damaged and it has deteriorated much more than it should have for my age. But it could have been worse. The people who found me were two young men who happened to be passing. One came to see me the next day at the hospital; he said they'd been worried I might die, and I thanked them effusively for their help. I asked about the first person that had been there, but he said that there was no one. I'd been lying alone on the ground, and it was only by chance that they had come down there, because one of them had left his bag in the car and they had returned to retrieve it. So no one could have known they were coming.

LUKE
Washington, USA

In 1969, I was driving from Seattle to San Francisco in my old station wagon. It was quite a hot day and I had the window open as I drove along. I came across a hitch-hiker, a longhaired boy holding his thumb out to hitch a ride. The sign he held up said San Francisco, so I stopped to allow him into the car.

We were a good few hundred miles from our destination at that point. As I drove, we talked, and I remember something strange in the way he looked at me. It was as if he could instinctively tell if I was lying and so I felt compelled to tell him the truth. You see, I was really on the run from Seattle. I had gotten my girlfriend pregnant and didn't know what to do about it, so I just left her behind and took off. I had no money and we'd had no plans to marry, and in the 1960s having an illegitimate child was quite a big thing.

The boy told me I should go back and face my responsibilities. We stopped for gas and to use the bathroom, and when I came out he had gone. There just seemed to be this seven-foot glowing tower in front of the station wagon. I heard the boy's voice again in my ear, telling me again to return to Seattle.

I did return to Seattle and married my girlfriend Mary three months later. We're still together and now have four lovely grandchildren. Mary said she had prayed and prayed that I would come back to her. I think the boy hitchhiker must have been some kind of angel answering Mary's prayers. I'm so glad that I went back. I still haven't met anyone quite like Mary. She was always the one for me, and I think the angels must have known it, too.

JANE, 36
London, England

Quite recently I was pushing my young son in his stroller near to where I live. There is a side road there that is quite wide, but with a curve close to the end where it meets a main road. I was walking along the main road, crossing the side road. I did take a look down it, but it is a one-way street, and if you can't immediately see a car coming you generally know that it is safe to cross.

Just as I got about halfway across, I heard a car coming, extremely fast. It all happened very quickly. I looked to my left and saw a red car coming faster than you would usually expect there, at the kind of speed you would expect on a motorway. I wasn't going to have time to get out of the way. I panicked and pushed the stroller as hard as I could, trying to at least get my son out of the way. I started to run after it, but I slipped and stumbled, and the stroller bounced horribly off the curb so that it was not clear of the road at all. If anything, it was even more likely to get hit.

I was staring at the approaching car when a man walked out from the sidewalk, quite deliberately, in front of it. I hadn't seen the man a moment earlier, but now he was stepping calmly in front of a speeding car. I realized I could hear a police siren and realized that the red car was being chased by the police, which was why it was going so fast.

The man was hit really hard by the red car and seemed to be thrown into the air. At the last moment, the driver tried to brake and swerve, and because of that he lost control and skidded. The car crashed hard into a lamp-post, which was half knocked down, and then bounced back into the road, coming to a halt only about ten yards away from me.

Meanwhile, I'd just managed to get back to my feet and ran toward the sidewalk, and a woman ran out and grabbed the stroller before I could get there and dragged that to safety, too. The driver of the red car had evidently been hurt in the collision and didn't get out. Three police cars pulled up in quick succession, and about ten policemen poured out and surrounded the car. I never found out who the driver was, but they obviously thought he was pretty dangerous; even though he was injured, they were treating him with real caution.

Then I realized that the man who had been hit must be injured. The fact that he had been hit had saved me or my son, or even both, from being hit by the speeding car. I desperately hoped that he wasn't dead. The impact had looked terrible. Slightly hysterical, I started gabbling about him to the woman who had helped get the stroller up on the sidewalk. She hadn't seen him, but I ran off to look for him while she watched my son for me.

He was nowhere to be seen. I managed to get some of the policemen to help me look, thinking he might have gone into a front garden or under one of the cars. We scoured the area, but there was no one there. No one seemed to have seen him except me and the driver of the car, who had crashed as a result. Later I learned that the driver died as a result of his injuries. I was angry at him for risking my son's life, but you wouldn't wish that on anyone.

Even so, that means I was the only one alive who had seen this man deliberately walk out and get hit. There wasn't a trace of him there or anywhere. I think the police thought I was just hysterical, but I definitely saw him, and it was because of him that the car diverted. I'm convinced it was an angel who didn't want me or my son to die that day.

Karen, 42
Washington, USA

A few years ago I was living in an old building in town with my girlfriend, Susie. The building wasn't very well maintained; the heat was always breaking down and the landlords were never in any hurry to fix it. A few times we had noticed the smell of gas in our apartment, coming from the old water heater that was in the hallway. We'd told the landlords about it, but all they did was send their maintenance guy round. He waved a few matches around and told us there was nothing wrong.

The problem came at the start of winter. I'm not sure if the boiler got worse or if it was because we'd had it on for a long time and also had all the windows closed. Susie and I had both been to work and then we'd come home and had some food in the kitchen. Afterward we sat in the living room, which opened onto the hallway, watching television. We were both pretty tired from work and I wasn't that surprised that we were both yawning. I had kind of a tight feeling in my chest but no more than that. Then I started feeling really sleepy and I lay back in the chair. Susie was doing the same thing, and I was vaguely wondering if we should turn the lights out and go to bed when I guess I fell asleep.

I'm not sure how long I was actually sleeping, probably an hour or so. But I was woken up by this very insistent voice, saying, "Karen, wake up, wake up now," over and over. I thought for a moment it was Susie, but it was a different voice—a voice I definitely recognized, although

I couldn't tell you who it was. I struggled to wake up. I felt really heavy and I couldn't breathe. The smell of gas was much worse than it had been, and I suddenly realized that it was the gas that had been putting us to sleep.

I managed to struggle to my feet, and I realized that Susie was slumped sideways on her chair. I shook her really hard and she hardly moved. I was feeling very dizzy now that I had stood up. I ran to the window and managed to get it open, and took a few really deep breaths of the cold air. Then I ran back and got my hands under Susie's shoulders and pulled her off the chair. She woke up slightly and grumbled, but I kept pulling her out through the hall to the kitchen. There was a door in the kitchen that opened to the outside. I put Susie on the floor and opened the door, then I pulled her head right outside in the cold air on the staircase and started shaking her again. Then she finally woke up.

We both had terrible headaches and our whole bodies felt a bit strange for a day or so, but there wasn't any lasting damage. That night we stayed with friends. Next day, we talked to the landlords and strangely enough they got the boiler fixed pretty damn quickly. It turned out that there was a leak, but also the extraction system was completely blocked, so all the gas escaping was backing up into our hallway. We'd been pretty lucky to survive, as people do die that way.

We moved out as soon as we could, anyway, as we both felt anxious in that apartment. Susie would never believe me about the voice. She thinks I was hallucinating because of the gas. But I know what I heard. It was someone whom I knew well, but have never met, who knew my name. And they saved us—it wasn't just luck that I woke up. There was more to it than that.

Martin, 39
Penrith, England

When I was twenty I had an experience up on the Pennines that convinced me that I have a guardian angel. I suppose we all have one, but that was the time I met mine. I had gone to walk up Cross Fell, which is the tallest of the hills in this part of the Pennines. I'd been up before, but never to the very top, so I set off early one Sunday in April. I knew enough to take a supply of water and food in my rucksack, but I was a bit underdressed; I had a sweater but no coat, as it was such a sunny day. It was a warm hot day at ground level, but it got a bit cooler as I walked up. There is a path that goes almost all the way to the peak, so all you have to do is follow that. Every now and then I would stop to look down on the countryside below; it's a fantastic view, across to the lakes and the peaks. There's no one up there but a few sheep, so it feels great to be there. I saw a few hawks below me, and even a hare, which is something you don't see very often.

At about 11:00 a.m. I saw a bank of cloud coming in from the west. That's always a slight worry on the Pennines, as the peaks are high enough that they are often completely covered by cloud. But I was only an hour or so from the top, so I decided to keep going. Not a very good decision, but there you go. I looked back now and then, meaning to turn back if the cloud got too close, but at the same time I was pushing myself to try and get higher. Finally, when I was probably no great distance from the top, I looked back and saw that the cloud was getting close.

Reluctantly I turned back and started walking down the hill. But the cloud was coming pretty fast, and soon it started coming down around me. It was like going from a sunny day to a dense fog within about ten minutes. It was very wet, cold fog, and I couldn't see more than about ten yards in front of my face. Just before it came down, I was on a part of the path that loops in a big curve around the edge of a scree slope. It seemed to me that if I went down the slope, I would get down the hill faster and couldn't miss the path.

Now this is the sort of thing you are told over and over not to do on the hills, but still, at that moment, I was sure it was the smart thing to do. So I went off the path and started making my way down this rocky slope. After about fifty yards, the light seemed to be getting a little better, and I vaguely saw the path about twenty-five yards away. But then I slipped on some loose stones and twisted my ankle. I was furious at myself for being careless, but it wasn't too bad. I could still walk, although it was going to be slower. So I set off again, and all the time the cloud seemed to be coming lower so it was getting darker again.

Where the path should have been, I found myself on a patch of rough grass. I could hear some sheep bleating in the distance, but I could hardly see a thing now. And I was really cold, shivering from the damp that surrounded me. I thought that I might have gone too far to the left, so I set off to the right, but then I seemed to be going back uphill, so I changed direction again and went downhill. But now the ground under my feet seemed to be getting muddy and boggy, and it was harder and harder to walk.

I was getting quite worried. Up until then I'd been sure I was okay, but now I knew I was lost. I was making slow progress, and for all I knew it was in the wrong direction. And you do hear stories of walkers dying of exposure or whatever up on the hills, so I was right to be worried.

Then I heard the voice. For a moment I thought it might just have been another sheep. But it was saying "This way," and it was definitely a person's voice. I shouted something like "Where are you?" but there was no answer. Then it just said "This way" again.

I peered through the fog, and to my left, where the voice was coming from, I thought I could just make out a white form, a kind of human figure. It was really hard to see in the fog, but I was sure there was someone there. It shouted to me again, a man's voice. I was certain that the path wasn't that way, but I didn't know what else to do, so I walked toward the voice. I was going slowly because of my ankle, but the ground was getting less boggy now. I came back onto a rocky area, which at least meant the ground was solid to walk on. And the voice stayed ahead of me, just out of reach, saying nothing but "This way." I kept catching a glimpse of the person, but it was always just at the point where visibility gave out.

It kept on that way for a few minutes, until I looked down and realized I was on the path. I was still in the fog, though, and the voice said "This way" one more time, so I set off along the path in that direction. It was up-hill, but only for a slight rise, and then the path started coming downhill again, quite steeply. After another ten minutes, the fog started to lighten. I was coming out of the clouds. It got to the point where I could see farther and farther ahead of me, but there was absolutely no one there. I could see about a half mile straight down the path and it was empty.

I was still really cold, but it was much better once I was out of the fog. As I limped down a bit farther, I could look back and see the bank of thick, dark gray cloud, not far above me. When I got to the bottom, it started rain-ing heavily again, so I got soaked one more time before I got back to the village where my car was. I ended up with a bad cold and a sore ankle, but nothing worse.

Later in the summer I went back up, not to the top (I've still never been to the top), but to see where I might have been while I was lost. I found the curved path and the scree slope. It's hard to be sure, but it looked very much as though I had actually managed to walk down the slope, across the path without realizing, and then into an open field. If I had been heading downhill from there, I would have been heading for some really boggy land, and beyond that there were several little rocky cliffs and crevices. So if that's where I'd been, I was going in the worst possible direction. I wish I'd seen the angel more clearly, but I'll always be grateful to him for helping me.

KARL, 56
Illinois, USA

When I started school, we used to go to and fro on a school bus—one of those old yellow buses. There was a woman called Mrs. Smith who tried to keep us all under control on the bus.

Once when I was six I missed the bus. I went to the end of the school path where we got picked up but I remembered I had left my painting behind. It was a painting I was particularly proud of, and I wanted to show my parents. I walked back to the art room and the teacher was still there, so I asked for my picture. He laughed and took a few minutes to find it in the drawer.

Then I walked back to the meeting place, but instead of a big group of children waiting, there was no one. The bus had come and gone and I had missed it. Mrs. Smith must have forgotten to check that everyone was there, or maybe she just assumed I was off school for some reason.

Now what I should have done was go back to the school and ask them to telephone my parents. But I felt embarrassed, as though it was a stupid thing I'd done and I had to do something about it. Honestly, it didn't even occur to me to go back into the school. I set off to walk back home. It was about two miles, a long way for a six-year-old. I knew the way because I had walked it once or twice with my mother, but I had never been out all alone like that before and it was a very frightening prospect.

I set off walking. I knew enough to cross roads at crossings, and I didn't get lost, but it was dangerous anyway. About halfway home was a particularly big highway, and I was standing there, trying to figure out how to get across. No one else seemed to be crossing, so I wasn't sure what to do. There was a break in the traffic so I tried to cross, but suddenly a car was coming. Someone grabbed me, picked me up, and ran across the road.

It was a man with dark hair. He told me that it hadn't been very clever of me to try and cross that road, and said he was going to take me home. He set off with me and he knew the way to my house. It was much faster once he was there. He helped me across the roads and took all the right turnings. It didn't occur to me at the time, I was only young, but I don't know how he could have known my address.

He took me to the end of my driveway and then told me to go to my parents. I walked up to the door and rang the bell, and when I looked back he was gone. My mother started crying when I opened the door. They'd been so worried when I wasn't on the school bus, they'd called the police and everything. I was still clinging on to my picture and I tried to give it to her, but she just grabbed me and hugged me. It was funny because it hadn't occurred to me that there was a problem until then.

Looking back, I wonder who the man was. It has always bothered me that he knew where I lived and didn't come to the door with me, so perhaps he was an angel who was there because I was in danger.

CARLA, 48
Illinois, USA

I was having an affair with a younger man. It all seemed glamorous and exciting; my marriage had been a little dull for a few years, perhaps because our children had grown up and left home. I did still love my husband in a way, but I just wasn't happy on some level, so when I met this younger man, I just let it happen. I felt sure my husband would find out soon, and I was letting it drift toward that. I was like a gambler—I knew sooner or later I was going to hit rock bottom, but I was just sitting and watching it all slide away.

One day I was lying there in bed in my lover's apartment, and I had what I can only describe as a vision. I was half asleep and I saw an angel come to fetch me. She took me with her and we flew over my house. I saw my husband at his desk, reading his newspaper. He is quite a solid, sensible man, but when the angel showed him to me, I somehow saw him in a different light. I realized that after all we had gone through and survived together, I was betraying him.

The angel brought me back to where I had been lying and left without a word. Suddenly, instead of feeling pleased with myself and excited, I felt dirty and ashamed. I vowed to change, and I did. I stopped seeing my lover and went "back" to my husband. That's to say I went back to being his faithful wife, as I had been for so long. And for whatever reason, it all started to work again. Finally, we got over the malaise that we had been in since the children left. Instead of treating each other as parents without children, we rediscovered each other as real people.

I tried to tell him once and a strange thing happened. He stopped me before I managed to say anything, and said that if I had anything bad in my past it was in the past— he didn't need to know. Then he told me a story about how an angel had come to him once. He had thought our marriage was falling apart and had been unhappy about it. He said that he had been willing the marriage to fail because he was bored, and he felt bad about that. Somehow the angel had shown him us as we used to be, and he had vowed to start again.

He said he wanted to forget all about the past—his past, my past—and start again. I couldn't help feeling he knew all about my infidelity and just didn't want us to have to talk about it. In a way, he might have been right to think that. It would only have been destructive. I might have felt I was confessing to clear the slate, but in a way my burden is that I have to live with the guilt of what I did and still try to make things work.

Somehow an angel helped us. We are much happier now than we were, and we have the angel to thank for that. I'm not sure why the angels chose to help us, but I can see that our lives would have been much more difficult if that hadn't happened.

DEIRDRE

Christchurch, New Zealand

I was abused for about a year when I was twelve. I don't want to tell you all the details, but it was my stepfather. When I told my mother about it, she refused to believe me and shouted at me for trying to spoil her happiness and drive her new husband away. It was horrible. Once my mother refused to listen, I just didn't know who else I could turn to. It kept happening, and I couldn't make it stop.

Afterward, I would often feel suicidal. After all, if I wasn't around any more, the problems would stop, for me and for my mother. But I also used to hear a voice speaking to me in my head. It was a woman's voice, speaking very slowly and precisely. It used to say that things wouldn't always be like this, and that I had to keep going. It was like someone trying to cheer me up, or at least stop me from doing anything stupid.

When I went back to school after the holidays, we had a new teacher, Miss McGuinness. As soon as she started, I liked her. School was a good thing at that time because I knew I was safe there. One day the teacher kept me behind after class. She asked me if everything was all right at home, because my grades had gotten much worse that year and a few of the other teachers had commented that I seemed distracted. I think most of them just put it down to adolescence, but she took the trouble to try to find out.

I couldn't tell her anything. I knew that telling someone outside of the family would be betraying my mother. So I just said nothing and left when she let me. But as I walked out and down the corridor, I heard the woman's voice in my head again. She was saying I had to tell Miss McGuinness. She said that the teacher would believe me, and that my mother would forgive me in the end, but that it was important for me to do something. I don't know if it was an angel or some other being protecting me. But these thoughts came to me totally from the outside. They were spoken in a way that I couldn't have spoken or thought myself, a very coherent, calm, adult kind of voice.

I went back and told Miss McGuinness. She was clearly very shocked and from there it all happened very quickly. The police were called and I went through a lot of interviews and bad things like that. It was terrible when the police took me home and arrested my stepfather. My mother was absolutely distraught and wouldn't talk to me. I ended up staying for weeks with my cousin, the nearest relative I had in town, but someone I didn't really know well.

My stepfather was never put in jail or anything. The evidence was just my word against his, and the police had to let him go. But for some reason, the whole thing made my mother realize that I hadn't made it up, and she kicked him out. He moved out of town, to my relief. I have never seen him again.

It took a long while before I was completely okay with my mother, but she realized I had to do something. I really think I might have killed myself or run away from home or something if I hadn't listened to that angel's voice in my head. It was a bad thing to have happen to me, in any case, and I find it hard to speak about it, but the voice helped me as well as it could in the circumstances.

GUARDIAN ANGELS

Jesus said that every child has an angel. Many of the accounts in this section involve the intervention of guardian angels in children's lives. Children do need more protection than adults. They are vulnerable, and as much as we try to protect them from all the bad things that might happen, there are always dangers and risks in the world. It seems that the angels may have a particular interest in protecting children.

There are also plenty of reports of guardian angels in adult lives. There is no reason to believe that the angels look after adults any less carefully than children. Perhaps it is just that children are less rigid in their thinking and more likely to recognize an angel when they meet one.

SARAH, 24
Michigan, USA

When I was young, about four or five, my parents used to fight a lot. Our apartment was very small and they would be arguing either in their bedroom or in the kitchen, right outside my bedroom door. The door would be open a crack, as I was scared of the dark, so I would even be able to see them going to and fro sometimes. It was always late, about midnight or later, after they had been drinking, so I'd be awakened by the shouting.

They used to say terrible things to each other. My mother would be saying how she wished she had never married him, and how badly she wanted to leave, and he'd be telling her to just go then. There would be smashing sounds as well, glasses and plates being thrown, I don't know by whom. And sometimes screaming, as they would even hit each other when it got really bad.

That's one of my first memories, and unfortunately it's a sad one. They split up eventually. I lived with my mother after that and my father would see me at weekends. It was better because they didn't fight anymore, but I was sad that my father wasn't at home.

When they were fighting, their voices sounded frightening. It was like someone horrible was pretending to be my parents, and they had the exact same voices except they were so angry and kind of distorted, which I guess was down to the drinking. It scared me, and I used to lie there with the pillow over my head so I couldn't hear so well.

I remember on several occasions that I felt a hand on my shoulder, and my angel would be there. I would look up and dimly see her looking down at me in the dark room while they were still shouting in the other room. She would stay there while I lay back down, and gently stroke my hair and shoulder until I went back to sleep. Often I would be awakened again later by my father, who used to come in to check that I was all right. He probably felt guilty about the noise and the things they'd been shouting. I used to tell him I'd been having a bad dream, which meant that he stayed to look after me for a while, but he'd still be tense and distracted. I liked it best when my angel looked after me, because I knew that she understood.

ALLY, 29
New York, USA

When I was about four, I went to the zoo with my uncle and aunt. I used to love the monkeys. We went straight there when we arrived and then we walked around the rest of the zoo. I couldn't understand why my uncle and aunt liked the aquarium so much, and while we were there, I got the idea that I should go back and see the monkeys.

I wandered off in that direction, meaning to go quickly and then come back. But I got lost and took a wrong turn. I ended up somewhere near the big cats. It took me about ten minutes to find my way back to the aquarium and when I got there, they were gone.

It's a terrible feeling when you get lost as a child. It didn't really occur to me that they would be looking for me. In fact, they were probably panicking themselves, as they were in charge of me for the day. But I just started running frantically around looking for them. I thought that maybe I should run outside and go find the car where they had parked it. But I would have had to cross the road, and I wasn't allowed to do that by myself.

Then a pretty lady stopped and asked if I was lost. I nodded and started crying. She took me by the hand and led me straight over toward the main buildings. There was an office or something there and my uncle and aunt were standing outside, looking worried. As we got there, the lady said, "There's your aunt and uncle." This was odd, because I hadn't told her who I was looking for, but she recognized them immediately. Why did she know who they were? That might have been explained by her being someone they knew but I didn't recognize. But then a year or two later, something similar happened.

I was shopping with my mother in the city. It was a very busy department store, and while she was looking at some cushions, I wandered off to look at the toys. But then I couldn't find her again. Again a lady found me, took my hand, and helped me find my mother. It was the same lady. That's why it is so strange. The only two times in my life I got lost like that, the same woman rescued me and made sure I didn't get into any trouble.

My mother was so angry at me that time, because she had been so scared, that I guess I finally learned not to wander off, so I don't remember ever getting lost again.

But I have a feeling that if I ever did really need her again, the lady would be there.

JASON
Birmingham, England

I saw an angel in my bedroom when I was about five or six years old. I woke up from a nightmare in which I was being chased and attacked by some giant bats. I was screaming and crying, and as I awoke I saw this tall, beautiful man standing at the end of my bed.

I didn't feel frightened of this man. He was so beautiful and seemed so gentle. I could see these huge shimmering wings behind him and he looked to be about nine feet tall. He held his arms out over me and said, "No harm can come to you." I immediately felt protected and loved. It was like being cuddled up in a really warm blanket on a cold, dark night.

I will never forget that feeling or what I saw that night. People have tried to tell me that I was still dreaming, but I feel in my heart that it was real. There was an angel in my bedroom that night, letting me know that I was cared about. So I do believe in angels; I have seen one with my own eyes.

BERNICE
Leeds, England

When my eldest daughter was a baby, about five months old I think, I remember something very weird happening. I was a single mum then; my husband had walked out before the baby was even born. He wasn't the type of man who could cope with responsibilities. I was always worried sick about how I was going to make things work all on my own.

On this particular day, I was cuddling and playing with my daughter as usual when I saw that something behind me had caught her eye. She had this huge amused smile on her face, and I turned around but there seemed to be nothing there. I looked back at her and made the little tickling noises she loved. As I was looking into her eyes, I could see my own reflection, but there also seemed to be something behind me, a very tall figure with the outline of what looked like wings. Again I turned round. I still couldn't actually see anything, although this time I felt that the world had been turned into a wonderful, loving space where my daughter and I would both be taken care of.

After that day, things began to work out. I got a good job where they were very understanding about time off because I had such a young baby. I also met my current husband later the same year. We've been together twenty years now, and I have another child with him. I like to think that what I saw that day was my daughter's guardian angel and that she's still being looked after, wherever in the world she goes.

GEORGE
Kentucky, USA

When I was about thirteen and my brother was eleven, we went to stay with our aunt and uncle on their farm because our mother was about to give birth to our sister.

They had a lot of livestock and it could be a noisy place. On top of that, their dog Herbert always slept on the floor of the spare bedroom, where we were sleeping, and he snored badly because he was an old dog.

I was finding it hard to fall asleep and could hear what I thought was thunder in the distance. Suddenly the bedroom was lit up in this really bright light. At first I thought it must be lightning, but it stayed too long to be that. I looked down at the end of my bed and there was a really tall man standing there, looking at me and my brother and smiling fondly.

The next morning I said nothing about it and things carried on as normal. It wasn't until about fifteen years later, when I was having a drink with my brother, that I brought the subject up. He said he had seen the same thing and had been keeping it quiet in case anyone would think he was crazy, or laugh at him. We think it was some kind of angel telling us that we were being looked after and protected.

BILLY
Manchester, England

When I was a kid, we used to play in the old derelict mills along the canal. We swung out over the canal on the old ropes that were used to haul things into the loading bays from the barges on the canal. We always dared each other to let go of the rope as we swung and jump onto the other side of the bank. Sometimes I'd feel brave enough to try it and other times I wouldn't.

One day, one of us lads fell into the canal. We knew he couldn't swim and we raced out of the mill to get over the bridge to the canal bank. We got to where he'd fallen in, and he seemed to float through the water to the side so that we could pull him out. After we'd got him out, he said he actually felt as if someone was in the water escorting him to safety. He hadn't swum or floated—more been pulled along by an unseen force. An angel must have been looking out for him that day.

ALISON
London, England

I'm convinced I had a visit from an angel a few years ago. I was working as a teacher at a very tough local school. The job was so stressful that I became depressed, and gradually my condition worsened until I had what I suppose you'd call a breakdown. I was at home actually considering taking a bottle of pills. It really had gotten that bad; I felt my life was no longer worth living.

Suddenly the room was filled with the scent of roses and I felt so calm and relaxed. I felt cared for, really; it was that kind of sensation. I went to bed that night and the next day at school applied for six months leave. During this time I worked as a volunteer in an orphanage in Kigali. The experience filled me with a sense of strength and capability. When I returned to London, I was a different person. I dealt with the stresses of teaching differently and in that way the experience changed my life.

EMILY
Amsterdam, Holland

I have been in a wheelchair since being hit by a car when I was nine years old. That was twenty years ago so I have become used to it. Whenever I go to our local grocery store, I always use the ramp and automatic doors at the side of the building so that I can get my wheelchair in.

One particular day I was heading for the ramp as usual when a woman came along the road and stopped me. She said hello and tried to engage me in conversation. I must confess I was a bit rude to her because I wanted to get on with my shopping and get home. Just as I was about to make my excuses and leave, there was an enormous bang. We both looked round and a bus had crashed into the side of the grocery store building. The ramp had been almost demolished.

I heard the woman saying, "See, you would have been there if it hadn't been for me." I turned around and she was already a long way down the road. I like to think that she was some kind of angel looking out for me.

TONI, 33
Greenwich, England

One of the weirdest things about walking through a tunnel is that every horror film you have ever watched comes crashing into your head. I worked for a few months as an usher in a theatre in the West End, which meant I didn't finish until about 11:00 p.m. After I'd got on a train full of happy people who had all, mysteriously, vanished by the time I got to my stop, I had to walk through Greenwich foot tunnel, on my own, to get home.

Every night I would hear my footsteps echoing through the tunnel and images of *Buffy the Vampire Slayer*, *The Evil Dead*, and anything I'd ever seen with clowns in it would seem to be in every shadow or noise. (I know to include clowns in that list is a bit odd, but I once saw a sketch at a circus that consisted of clowns pulling very large teeth out of each other and I've never quite got over it.) Anyway, with my hyperactive imagination and the fact that it actually was quite late and just a little bit eerie, I used to dread my journeys home.

About the third time I did this supernatural walk through the tunnel, I noticed a guy walking just ahead of me. Not having a handy wooden stake, silver bullet, or whatever it is that's needed on this kind of occasion, I just walked a little slower. He seemed to slow his pace, too, but not enough to make me want to curl up in a ball and start wanting my mother, so I kept walking. When I got to the end he had gone—back to his castle in Transylvania, I presumed.

The next night, gritting my teeth once more against the horrors awaiting me, I noticed he was there again. I slowed, hoping he wouldn't notice the one other person in the entire tunnel with really loud shoes. By the time I got to the end of the tunnel, he had disappeared. This continued to happen, night after night, until in the end I didn't slow my pace and started to look for him. He was always there, always guided me home, and always disappeared. When the job finished, I remember thinking how much I would miss the money, and also that I wouldn't see him again.

A few months later, I had been out with some girl-friends and was just slightly the worse for wear. I wandered in a not altogether straight line into the tunnel and decided to find him but, no matter how slowly I walked, he never appeared. I can't lie; I felt a bit let down. Then, just as I reached the mouth of the tunnel, I could see him leaning against the arch at the end. I felt so relieved that he hadn't left me to the werewolves that it took me until the next day to realize that, like my mother, my guardian angel didn't approve of drinking.

CRISSY, 40
Colorado, USA

I was fascinated that my toddler seemed to know exactly what angels are. One day my friend sent me a Christmas card. It had a lovely picture of an angel on it. It wasn't one of those really fancy ones with halos and angels. The wings were there, but were quite small, and the main thing was that it was a beautiful woman in white, with light all around her.

I showed it to Matty, who was just three, and said, "Look at the lovely angel." And he said, "Yes, she comes here sometimes, doesn't she?" I thought it was just one of those cute things kids say. But he kept on about it, saying that the angel came in the night and she was sometimes there when I wasn't.

One incident really persuaded me that he might be telling the truth about it. I was in the kitchen and he was reaching for the bottles under the sink. I told him firmly that he mustn't play with them, and he knew this anyway. A few weeks before, I had left him alone for a moment in the kitchen to answer the telephone, and when I got back, he had somehow managed to get the top off the bleach. Maybe I hadn't put it back on properly, but I was quite scared. It was just sitting there beside him, open, and he could have drunk it or knocked it over or anything. I shouted at him and told him never to play with the bottles. At the time he mumbled something about a lady.

This time when I scolded him about the bottles, he said that the angel had told him not to drink them. I asked if that was when I had scolded him about them before, and he said, "Yes, the angel told me not to, so I didn't." So I think maybe the angel had already saved him from doing anything stupid, in the moments before I got back to him, because it's strange for him to take the top off and then just put it down. Toddlers are so inquisitive, if no one told him to stop, he would have just kept going and tried to see what else he could do with the bottle—drink it, pour it out, or whatever came into his head. But instead he just put it down safely upright and walked away.

When they get to that age they can be so difficult to look after. They are like little monkeys, the way they go around poking their faces into everything. I have often thought it's a miracle that Matty never got hurt, but the more I think about it, the more I think we had a bit of help.

Matty's five now, and he doesn't talk about the angel any more. But I hope she is still there if he ever needs her. I'll do my best to look after him so she doesn't need to help, but the terrifying thing with children is all the different dangerous things in the world they are going to come across. All you can do is pray that they are safe, and hope that if you ever need it, you get some help.

MATTHEW
Oban, Scotland

We used to play in the loch as boys and often we'd try to swim out as far as we could, floating and diving and daring each other to go deeper. One day one of our friends, Donald, dived very deep and didn't resurface. We dived down to try and look for him, but the loch is very deep and we couldn't find him. We thought he must have drowned.

We were crying and frightened and made our way back to shore to tell someone what had happened. Donald was sitting on the shore with an old fisherman who he said had taken him into his boat and brought him to shore. None of us in the water had seen any fishing boat nearby that day and we never saw the old man in the area again. I think Donald was saved that day by a higher force, possibly an angel.

ANDI, 34
Helsinki, Finland

My first child was born two years ago—a girl called Elle. When she was a tiny baby, she slept in our room in a straw basket. I used to be terrified that she would stop breathing in the night. You hear frightening things about crib death, and she was so little and fragile I just couldn't believe that she was strong enough.

We were having trouble sleeping anyway, because she liked to be held when she was falling asleep, so one of us would have to hold her for a long time. Then, three or four hours later, she would be crying for milk and my wife would have to get up. After a few weeks, we moved on to bottles of milk for the night, but even so it was difficult.

On top of this, every time I woke up, or just as I was about to fall asleep after being woken, I would panic that I couldn't hear her breathing. I would have to get up and go over to the basket and turn the light on, so that I could see her little chest rising and falling. Then I would go back to sleep. We were getting exhausted and my wife was getting infuriated that every time she fell asleep, she would be awakened, either by the baby or by me fumbling in and out of bed so I could check on her. I knew it was a silly fear, but it became compulsive at one point. Then one night I fell asleep with the light on, and I woke as usual an hour or so later, with my heart pounding, panicking that I had to check on Elle.

I started to get up and looked across the room. There was an angel sitting in the chair next to Elle's basket. She was a young woman with a very kind face. She looked up and smiled at me and put her finger to her lips. Then she looked back down at Elle and just sat there. I realized she was letting me know that Elle was being looked after. I sank back and went back to sleep.

I still worried about Elle, of course, but after that I realized I was only making things worse by worrying so, and I managed to get a bit more sleep. When you get through those first few months and start being allowed to sleep through the night again, it all turns into a bit of a blur. You were so tired all the time, you can't remember every detail. But at the time it is strange. It is a beautiful time because you have this amazing gift of a new little person. But it is also terrifying and physically very demanding. No one can go for long without a proper night's sleep without starting to get run down and emotional.

I knew raising a child was never going to be easy, but the angel helped at a moment when I was only making things more difficult for myself. I told my wife about it recently. At the time I didn't want to mention it, but then recently we were talking about that time and I told her about the angel. And you know what she said? She just said, "Of course. I always knew she was there. I saw her the very first night in the hospital, looking down at Elle when she was asleep." If only she'd told me that at the time, maybe I would have slept better myself!

MARJORY, 41
London, England

When I'm on my way home from work, I walk past a school. The road is always crowded with mums and a few dads waiting to pick up their kids. I finish work earlier

than most people because I'm the office assistant for a local building firm and I have to start when the contractors
come in. That means being at the office by 7:30 in the
morning.

I don't mind starting that early; I've never had a problem getting up in the morning, unlike my two teenage
children. I'm glad it's my husband and not me who has to
deal with hauling that pair out of bed! It also means that
I always get a little bit of daylight at the end of the day,
even in the winter, and that I'm home on my own for an
hour or so before the house goes mad again.

Anyway, normally when I pass the school, it's just before going home time and the kids are all still in their
classrooms. But sometimes, if I've stayed a bit late or
picked up some milk or bread from the shop, I go past
when most of the parents have been and gone and there's
just a few kids left in the playground, waiting for the late
arrivals.

There's always a few parents that don't quite get there
on time. I did it myself when my kids were little—the car
won't start or there's a phone call just as you're leaving or
something. The school always leaves a teacher in charge
until the last child has been collected, so it's perfectly
safe.

I'm a bit of a nosy old bag, so I usually have a look to
see if it's the same kids being picked up late every time
and, more often than not, that's what happens. Busy
parents, I suppose, or just plain irresponsible. Recently,
though, I've been looking much more closely, because I

started to become aware of some other figures in the playground who aren't kids or the teacher. The first time I saw them, I wasn't really paying attention and I caught a glimpse of what I thought were older children, one with each of the little ones, and I thought that the school must be trying out some kind of scheme to keep the kids happy while they were waiting for their mums and dads to arrive.

It was only when I got home that I remembered that the school only teaches up to the age of eleven. The people I'd seen had looked much bigger than that, so the next day I deliberately left work a bit late again, and when I passed the school, I stopped to have a closer look. The older kids were there again, one with each of the little ones, but I found it hard to get a good look at them, or to make out their faces very well. It's not that it was getting dark or anything; it's just that I didn't seem to be able to focus on them for any length of time.

I also noticed that the little kids weren't aware of the older ones, perhaps because they never seemed to speak, even though they were never more than a couple of feet from the child they were looking after. And, whenever a child's mum or dad arrived to take them home, the caretaker just disappeared. I never actually saw them vanish in a puff of smoke; they were simply there one minute and not the next.

I've passed the school at that time on lots of occasions now, and the older ones are always there. I can see them a little more clearly now and there always appears to be a vague glow around them, a bit like the way streetlights look in the winter when it's just getting dark.

I'm pretty sure that I'm able to see the children's guardian angels, making sure that they're safe until the parents turn up. I haven't ever taken anybody else to see this because I'm not sure that the angels would approve and, anyway, I don't think anyone else would be able to see them. I don't know why I can see them, but I feel very lucky to be allowed to. I always leave work that bit later now, just so I can see the angels. My boss thinks it's because I'm finally taking my job seriously, but what does he know?

ALISON, 18
Michigan, USA

My dad was in the army. He used to be away for a few months at a time on missions, but I'd be fine with my mother, and she'd tell me how my daddy loved me and how much he missed me.

The one time I got really scared was when he went away to the first Gulf war, after Iraq invaded Kuwait. I was just old enough to understand where he was going and that people get killed in wars. I started to get really scared in the middle of the night. I would wake up and stare at the ceiling and imagine terrible things. I'd seen horrible things on the news, and no matter what my mother said, I was terrified that I wasn't going to see him again or that he was going to get hurt in some terrible way. My mother knew I was worried and upset, but

I think she wasn't that happy herself at that stage, and it was difficult for us both.

One night I woke up and started worrying again. I got up and went downstairs to get myself a glass of water and there was a strange woman sitting at the kitchen table. She told me to sit down, and then she held my hand and told me that my father was going to be fine and that he knew I was worrying about him. She said it was only natural for me to worry, but that I had to be brave for the sake of both my parents. Then she gave me a lovely hug and just held me there for a while.

I slept much better after that. Next day I remembered what she had said, and I went up to my mother and gave her a hug too. I thought about how nice it had been for me and thought that maybe she needed a hug too. I told her that an angel had told me daddy would be okay and she just started crying and crying. I was quite shocked. I hadn't really realized how scared she was until then. After that, we probably supported each other a bit better, rather than tiptoeing around trying to pretend everything was fine.

My daddy was okay in the end, although he had a lucky escape when a rocket landed right next to his vehicle but didn't explode. When he got back, he said that the angels had been with him, and that not everyone had been so lucky. I was glad when, in the end, he left the army and stayed home.

Terry, 34
Worthing, England

I'm a cab driver and I work nights, which means that I end up doing a lot of trips to the airport in the early mornings after all the fares from late nightclubs have dried up. Where I live, the trains don't get started until about six in the morning, but the first flights, for business and for holidays, take off at about the same time.

As it happens, I like driving at that time of the day because the roads are pretty clear and there aren't as many crazy people out there. It's around forty miles to the airport and then, of course, forty miles back. When I've come in to work at eight or nine at night, which is a normal shift for me, I often finish by doing those last forty miles after I've been in the driver's seat for ten or twelve hours and I'm exhausted.

It's easy to lose a bit of concentration or just drift into your own thoughts when you're cruising along at seventy miles an hour—and obviously that's not a good idea when you're in control of a ton of metal. One time, I think I might have fallen asleep for a few seconds. All I know is that I was suddenly speeding along the hard shoulder of the motorway and knocking over two or three traffic cones that were lined up on the side of the road. It was truly frightening. I stopped to try and get myself back together and I can clearly remember wishing with all my might that I had someone friendly in the passenger seat to keep me company on those sorts of trips.

The next time I did one, a few days later, I took a couple who were on their way to Spain for a couple weeks. They were half asleep—their flight was at 6:15—but they gave me a nice tip and woke up a bit when we reached the airport. They were obviously excited at the thought of their holiday and, to be quite honest, I was a bit jealous.

I drove out of Departures and got back onto the motorway for the journey home. About halfway back, I was starting to get tired again when a voice from the passenger seat said, "Terry, you should stop for a bit. Get a cup of coffee." As you can imagine, I was a bit alarmed. It certainly woke me up. I looked across and there was a man in the seat staring straight ahead out of the windscreen. He looked a bit like my uncle Joe, who runs a trucking company in Brighton, but it was hard to tell because I was trying to keep my eyes on the road. In fact, it was hard to make him out at all, and I started to worry that I actually had fallen asleep and was dreaming all this.

I pulled over and the man said, "Not here, mate. You should find some coffee." I'm not sure what I said, but I knew he was right, so I drove another mile down the road to a service station. When I'd stopped the car again, I looked at him and asked who he was. He turned his head to me and I noticed that, even though he still reminded me of Joe, I kind of stopped registering his face because he had the most piercing, clear gray eyes I had ever seen. He said, "I'm here to keep you safe, Terry."

I believed that he was. I'd never had any truck with people that went to mediums or did any of that spiritualist stuff before, but here it was, happening to me. I think I wished for an angel that time when I'd nearly killed myself and one came along, took pity on me, and sat in the car with me for the long drive home.

He stayed all the way back, but he was gone by the time I'd gotten out of the car outside my house and went around to the passenger door to see if he was real. He's joined me quite a few times since then and he never says much, but he likes some of the music I listen to on the local oldies station. I thought for a bit I might be going mad, but I told my girlfriend about him, and she said that I should be grateful for any help I could get. She said he sounded like a nice guy, and when I said that I thought that he was some kind of angel, she said that she thought he probably was.

Mary

Australia

My husband left me when I was pregnant with our second child. Things had been bad between us, and I knew he'd had an affair. Stupidly, I thought that when I got pregnant it would make things better, but it actually made them worse. He wanted me to get rid of it, which is something I could never do. Then he got angry and started accusing me of trying to trap him and all this terrible stuff came out. In the end he went off with the other woman, the one he'd had the affair with. I was left on my own. I had my mother and sister living close by, so they helped all they could, but I was dreading the future.

I'd been quite depressed after Jon, my eldest son, was born. It probably didn't help our marriage because my husband was no use at all. He just thought I ought be able to cope single-handedly with it all and got angry if I started crying or telling him how bad I felt. I had finally gotten over it, but now I knew I had to go through it all again, and this time I really would be on my own. I had no idea how I would cope with Jon and with a daughter (I'd had the scans and knew it was a baby girl that was due).

About a month before the due date, I was cleaning the kitchen and Jon was playing out in the garden. I was once again fretting about how I was going to cope with him. I looked out and saw that there was a woman following him around. She was sitting in the swing chair watching him, and then when he went over toward the gate that led out to the road she would go over and stand in front of it. He didn't seem to know she was there. He would have been three at that point, full of energy and new ideas, and a real handful. But this patient woman was just calmly following him round, making sure he didn't get into any trouble.

She looked up and smiled straight at me, a lovely warm smile. I went out to see who she was and to say hello, but when I got outside she wasn't there. Or if she was still there, she was invisible. I realized that she had been letting me know that I wouldn't be on my own after all, that she would be there to help with Jon. I felt a bit silly but I stood there in the garden thanking her and talking to her about how worried I'd been. And even though I couldn't see her, I was sure she understood.

My waters broke that night, and my mother had to come and look after Jon while I went to the hospital. Kim was born at about noon, a beautiful little girl. After I got home I did feel a bit down at times, but any time things got too hard, I used to talk to Jon's angel and tell her about it. I never saw her again, but knowing she was there helped more than I can possibly say.

ADRIAN, 34
Bournemouth, England

When I was eight, I flew to Italy on my own. It sounds strange, but I was going to see my grandmother and aunts and uncles over there. My mother and father took me to the airport and made sure I got there safely. All the cabin crew knew I was on my own and helped out.

Before I got on the plane, I was fine. And even when I sat down, I wasn't scared. All the attendants kept coming and checking if I was all right, and I kept saying yes. I'd flown before, as we had been on holiday in Europe a few times, so I thought I'd be okay. But then, when we started taking off, I started to get scared. There's that moment when the plane starts going faster and faster, and without my mum or dad there to explain what was happening, I started worrying about what was going on. Then, after we got up in the air, there were some sharp banks and turns that felt very alarming. I started to get more and more upset, but I didn't want to make a fuss and ask for any help so I just sat there in my seat.

It got worse, about half an hour into the flight, when the captain asked us all to put our seatbelts on because there was some turbulence coming up. I'd never experienced turbulence before and I was terrified. I thought it meant that we might crash. I'd seen disaster movies, so I knew planes could crash. The attendants did check on me, but they were pretty busy going round making sure everyone was okay.

Then a man came and sat down next to me. He made sure my seatbelt was fastened and did his own up. He asked if I was scared, and I said, "Yes, a little bit." He started to explain to me about turbulence and what was going to happen. He said the plane would suddenly drop, and that it would be a bit like being on a rollercoaster. He asked if I'd been to the fairground and gone on the rides. I said yes, and he explained that it would feel a bit like that: a bit alarming, but basically safe. He told me that turbulence couldn't really hurt you on an airplane so long as you were belted in safely, and that really it was kind of fun.

Then the turbulence started, and it was quite bad. There were a few quite bad drops and you wouldn't have been able to walk around. But now that the man had explained to me what was happening, I was much less scared. He kept telling me when there was about to be another big one and it ended up being almost fun.

Eventually it was over and he went back to sit in his own seat. I was fine for the rest of the journey. When we got to Rome and landed, I thought I ought to tell him thank you for helping. I was at the front of the plane, so I was first or second off. I waited there for the man to come past so I could thank him, but no one who looked anything like him got off. I waited right till the end but he definitely wasn't there. Whoever it was, it was very kind of him to help me, because I would have had a terrible time otherwise.

MOLLY, 73
London, England

I grew up in London during the Blitz. I lived in Stoke Newington, Dalston, not too far from the East End, which was a major target for the bombers. It was an interesting time to grow up. Of course, the adults found it very frightening, but as a child it was like all the rules were suspended. You didn't really understand that that wasn't normal life, and no matter how much of a cliché it is, everyone did look out for each other. There was a great spirit.

I was evacuated, but I had a terrible time with the family I was sent to stay with. I hated the countryside and they treated me quite badly. I ran away and came back to London. On the train back to London, there was a man who sat opposite me. He knew that I was an evacuee going back to town—I thought it must be obvious. He talked to me on the way back, and at Paddington he took me to a taxi and made sure that the taxi driver knew where to take me. It seemed very kind of him, but people did a lot of kind things for strangers in those days.

My family wasn't very pleased to see me. It wasn't that they didn't like me or anything, but I was just one more thing for them to worry about. They wanted me to go back but I refused, so they set about trying to find a new place for me to go. They arranged for me to stay with some distant cousins, but they couldn't take me for a couple of weeks.

A few days later, I was out playing in the street when I saw a man with a horse pulling a cart. I loved horses, so I followed after it. I knew my way around pretty well, but I wasn't really concentrating and I got lost a few streets away from home. I stopped following the horse and set off back home, but went the wrong way and ended up somewhere over near Shoreditch, a long way from home.

That's when the sirens went off for a bomb raid. They didn't usually come in the afternoon but for some reason they did that day. I was really scared, not knowing how to get home fast enough to get into the shelter in the garden with my father. Then a man stopped to help me. It was the same man who had been on the train, by some strange coincidence. He was a dark-haired man, very tall, with blue eyes, in a dark suit. He took me up to one of the nearest houses and asked them to look after me. They were a nice family and were quite happy to look after a nine-year-old. The man told me not to worry about my family; he'd let them know. He didn't know me but he said that anyway.

Meanwhile, my dad was going mad looking for me. He was running up and down the street where we lived, trying to see where I'd gotten to. It was long after the time when he should have got into the shelter, but he didn't want to go in until he found me. He would have never forgiven himself if I had gotten hurt or killed. A man came and told him I was all right, in a shelter, and that he should get inside. He told me later it was a tall man with dark hair and blue eyes. It sounded very much like the man who had helped me, but it was so far away, he couldn't possibly have helped me and then got to my dad in time.

My dad went into the shelter, still worried about me but hoping what the man had said was right. He asked the man if would come in too, but he just said he would be fine and walked off down the street, in the middle of an air raid. About five minutes later, a huge bomb landed on our street. It didn't hit our house, but it fell in the middle of the road, making a massive crater and blowing out all the windows. One house was damaged too badly and had to be knocked down. My dad would have been killed if he'd still been out there.

I think that the man was an angel, and that his main aim was to save my dad, because my dad would have taken the chance and stayed out there otherwise. As it was, he was badly shaken. I was taken home by the mother of the family I stayed with, after the all clear, and he was shouting at me and crying with relief at the same time. It was only later that he told me about the man who had saved him and I worked out that it was the same man who had helped me on two separate occasions.

I went to stay with the cousins in the end and it was fine. We were lucky not to lose anyone in our family in the Blitz, but we knew plenty of people who weren't so lucky.

HANK
Oregon, USA

Once I was driving my truck down a country road near where I live. I was going at a reasonable speed and coming up toward a long curve when I saw a car coming up fast behind me. It was some guy in too much of a hurry, who kept trying to pull out and get a look so he could pass me. The view ahead was not good because it was summer and there were trees to either side, but this guy was in too much of a hurry to wait until a safer place. He just hit his horn to let me know he was coming and set off.

I was shaking my head and slowing down a bit when I looked back at the road ahead and saw a kid coming out from a path on the left-hand side, looking the opposite way down the road. He was looking for cars coming the other way but apparently it didn't occur to him to check back in our direction.

The guy overtaking me saw him too and started braking, but there wasn't enough space for him to stop. He was right beside my big truck on a narrow curve, so there was no space for him to swerve around the kid. It was like watching something horrible in slow motion. The car was heading straight for this kid and only at that moment did he start to turn his head and look round at us.

At that instant I saw something bizarre. The kid jolted in the air, twisted, and fell back toward the side of the road. The only way of describing it is to say that it was like someone invisible pushed him. He didn't jump, but his feet left the ground and he was thrown to the grass beside the road. The overtaking car only just missed him, but at least it did miss him.

I was already braking, so I slowed down and stopped. The guy in the passing car just sped up and drove away, which I thought was shameful. I ran back to make sure the kid was okay. He was just standing there, staring down the road. I asked him what happened and it seemed like he had no idea, but he knew he'd had a lucky escape. He was about twelve and, at the speed that guy was going, he easily could have been killed.

LIONEL
Cornwall, England

I come from a fishing family and there are plenty of stories about angels. It's said that an angel came to my great-grandfather when he was out in the boat, and because of that he knew to hurry home. His wife nearly died in childbirth, and if he hadn't got home to get help, she almost certainly wouldn't have made it.

You sometimes see angels above a boat in a very bad storm. My father used to tell me not to look at them. He thought it was bad luck to see them, as they might be coming to take you if you died. But I always thought, how could it be bad luck to see an angel? And I used to look out for them. Several times, in a really bad storm, as we were trying to keep the vessel under control, I've looked up through the driving wind and rain, and through the spray of the waves, and seen two angels in the rigging. They weren't holding on to anything, just hovering there. They weren't easy to see—it's hard to see anything in a real storm. But I could see the light from their bodies, and occasionally I could catch a glimpse of their faces. I didn't look for too long, though. My father would be right about it being bad luck if you let yourself get distracted. You've got to keep your wits about you to survive out there in the bad storms. Thankfully, I've never been hurt or had a boat go down. If I have the angels to thank for that, then I am very grateful.

MARY, 62
Massachusetts, USA

I used to feel bad about leaving my mother alone when she was ill. She was very frail, and sometimes when I was working she had to cope at her house by herself; my father had died a few years earlier. She had to get up and down the stairs even to use the toilet and make a hot drink. She wasn't too ill to do that but it tired her out, especially in the winter when everything seems a bit harder. So she spent a lot of time in her bedroom, sitting up in bed reading or watching this little portable television I'd bought for her.

But my mother had a few friends who came round to help. She lived in a different neighborhood than me and had made new friends there, some of whom I hadn't met. I was glad about that, as it made me feel less guilty about not being able to do more. I used to get there in the evening and ask what she'd been doing, and often she would say, "It's fine. Elsa's been here all afternoon sitting in the chair. We've been talking." I never met Elsa, but she always seemed to come round when no one else could make it and sit with my mother in the afternoon.

Later on, my mother fell and broke her hip and had to go into the hospital. I took as much time off work as possible to visit, but again, it was always Elsa who had been to visit her earlier in the day, who had been talking with her. Once I talked to the nurse and she said that no one had been to visit my mother all day, even though my mother had said that Elsa had been there. I was actually angry because I thought my mother was patronizing me, making up a visit so that I wouldn't feel like she was being neglected. But she just kind of laughed and said, "Sorry I never explained, but Elsa's an angel. She looks after me." I really didn't know what to say. I didn't want to argue, and my mother looked so serene when she explained this that I felt like, no matter what the truth of it was, it was something I shouldn't interfere with.

Right up until she died a few years later, she would go on mentioning Elsa and I never argued about it. Then, when she died and I had to organize the funeral, I had to ask all her friends if they knew Elsa so I could ask her to the funeral. And none of them had even heard the name. There didn't seem to be a real person of that name. The more I thought about it over the years, the more convinced I've become that my mother was telling the truth.

GARETH, 55
New Hampshire, USA

Whenever I have some time off work, and on the weekends, I like to go hiking in the woods. There's lots of places near my home where you can get into the woods and I normally don't have to drive for more than an hour or so before finding a track or a dirt road that I can wander along for a few hours and forget about work and money and all the other little daily worries.

Those walks are what keep me sane, I think. The only trouble is that I'm not very good with directions and so I have a tendency to get lost with alarming regularity. Nowadays, my wife tries to make me take my cell phone with me, but I don't like the idea that anybody could just call me up in the middle of the wilderness, especially my mother—she's got a good heart and she's getting older now, but she can talk forever about nothing.

So I generally leave the phone in the car—that way I've taken it and my wife's happy, but I don't have to answer it. Most of the times when I've gotten lost, it wouldn't do me any good anyhow. If you don't know where you are, how can you call someone and ask the way back?

Usually I just blunder around for a while and end up back on a bit of pathway that I recognize, or I see some houses or something and then I'm okay. A few times, however, I've started to get really worried, often when it's getting near dark and I can't figure out where I am or how I'm going to get out of the trees, and that's when I've been guided by what I like to think is an angel.

He doesn't look like you might imagine an angel to look; he looks more like me. He's got hiking boots and a small haversack and he wears a bright red jacket (although I prefer yellow, myself). I always see him when I'm just about reaching the end of my tether and have been trying to work out the way back to the car for at least an hour.

Rather annoyingly, I've never been able to speak to him. He appears about a hundred yards from where I am and waves to me to come his way, but when I get to where he was, he's another hundred yards away, waving again. This always continues, him waving and disappearing and me following, until I suddenly stumble on my car.

The first time it happened, it was late October, freezing cold and, by the time I'd reached the car, nearly dark. I'd been very scared that I was going to end up stuck out in the woods all night and die of exposure. I was so grateful to my mysterious rescuer that I got even colder trying to find him to thank him. I looked all over the place where my car was parked, but there were no houses or other vehicles around and there was absolutely no sign of him.

The second time it happened was in midsummer, but I was no less frightened; I'm not an experienced woodsman and find the idea of snakes and animals scary. He appeared again, led me to safety and then, once again, was nowhere to be found. I thought it must be an extremely odd coincidence that time but, when it happened for a third time, I began to wonder what this was all about.

Since then, he's arrived every time I've gotten myself lost, about ten or twelve times in all, and he's always gotten me out of trouble. I believe that he's some kind of angel of the woods who comes to the rescue of the directionally challenged. I don't think it's just me that he helps; I think he's there for anybody who's not sure where they are and are a little bit worried about it. Perhaps he's one of the mountain men that first explored this area who's carrying on with what he used to do and guiding innocents through the forest. I don't know. I do know that, if it weren't for him, I would surely have spent at least one cold and lonely night on my own in the woods by now. So to me, at least, he's an angel who watches out for the unwary or, in my case at least, the foolish.

Angus, 32
New Jersey, USA

I was going away on a business trip, and for the first time since our daughter Helena had been born, my wife was coming with me. My mother was looking after Helena. She knew her well and they were staying at our home, so I knew it was all going to be fine. But on the other hand, my wife and I were flying together and we were both scared because we thought that, if something did happen to the airplane, our daughter would be an orphan. This was a very upsetting thought, of course.

The week before, at my mother's suggestion, I had written a will, and as part of it I had written a letter to Helena, to be opened in the event that we died and to be shown to her when she was old enough to understand. Of course, it is impossible to say everything you want to in a letter like that, but I wrote a few pages telling her how much we had loved her and how happy I was to have her in my life. I also wrote that I would be proud of her no matter what she chose to do, so long as she was true to herself.

It was very strange writing a letter like that, because I was forced to put myself in a position where it came true, and my daughter aged eight or ten was reading a letter from her father who had died. I wept a few tears while I was writing it, not of self-pity or pure sentimentality, but just because it brought home to me how enormous the family bond is, and how my life had been transformed by the change from being a married couple to being a family.

As we drove off, my mother came out to the front stoop with Helena and they waved goodbye to us. Behind them in the hall, I could see a white figure, a man or woman, watching them calmly as they waved to us. I knew for certain that there was no one in the house, so I immediately thought that it must be an angel, and it made me so happy to think that there was an angel watching out for them. Of course, the trip was fine and nothing went wrong, but it was an interesting and revelatory experience nonetheless.

There were two other times I saw evidence of angels. Once I bought an old Polaroid camera as a toy and took pictures of my family. In two of them, as the image started to form, I could clearly see the figure of a woman standing behind Helena. It was very distinct and I shouted for my wife, but as the picture set, the figure faded both times, leaving only Helena. It drove my wife crazy but I'm sure I saw something.

The last time was when Helena was not much older, about five, and we went on holiday to Mexico. The airport was very busy when we arrived and we were all tired from the flight. Then we found out we had to wait for a coach to transfer us to the hotel, and that it might be an hour's wait. This was the last straw for Helena, who started crying and having a tantrum. She had mostly outgrown tantrums, but occasionally they came back at times like these. I was trying to calm her down and she just sat down a little distance away, still crying.

At that moment I saw that another family, who were walking toward us with a luggage cart, were headed toward her. The wheel of the cart was going to roll straight over her hand. She didn't see it coming, and it was a huge, heavy cart laden down with suitcases, and I could see that the man pushing it hadn't seen that he was about to crush Helena's hand.

I was watching this as though it was in slow motion, too far away to get there in time. Then, at the very last minute, Helena's hand was snatched away. I say snatched for good reason. It jerked as though it was out of her control, and she looked as surprised as me that her out-stretched arm had moved. The cart passed by and missed her by a fraction. The man saw what he had nearly done and apologized profusely. I was just relieved that Helena was all right and extremely grateful to whomever, to the invisible hand that had intervened to help her. I tend to think that it would be the same invisible hand that helped look after her the first time we went away, and probably countless other times I can't even guess about.

JACQUES
Lyons, France

I was driving home along the highway at about 7:00 p.m. one evening when I came across a roadblock and had to divert off the highway for a while before I could get back on it. I finally got back on the highway past the block-age and carried on home. I got home about 7:35 p.m. My wife greeted me with such relief that I thought something must have happened. She said there had been a huge ac-cident on the highway, causing a massive pile-up. Many people had been killed. I later found out that the accident had happened at around 7:05 p.m., but the roadblock had not been put in place until around 7:25 p.m.

I can't explain it. My wife thinks angels guided me home to her that night. What we're both sure about is the times at which these things happened. I was defi-nitely home at 7:30 p.m.

Melanie
Sydney, Australia

My first husband was a very aggressive and violent man. Often I would go to bed and leave him drinking downstairs. I would lie awake worrying that when he'd finished drinking, he'd come upstairs and take all his anger out on me.

On this particular night, I woke up to find a very tall woman standing at the foot of my bed. She had the whitest blonde hair I had ever seen and seemed to be about seven feet tall. Her dress seemed to sparkle in this really dazzling way. Before I had fallen asleep, I had prayed that my husband would not treat me violently. Now this woman seemed to be holding her arms over my head and willing kind thoughts upon me. The whole room was lit with peace and I knew that I would be able to sleep safely that night.

Eventually I gathered up the courage to leave that husband. I think it was first seeing the angel in our bedroom that made me able to think about standing on my own two feet. It felt as if the angel was saying, "I will protect you tonight but you can do this on your own." I could and I did.

Keith, 40
Birmingham, England

My wife sees angels when she sleepwalks. It is quite unsettling. She is a terrible one for sleepwalking. I'll often wake up to find her blundering around the room, looking like she's awake, but actually completely asleep and a bit confused. She will be trying to open an imaginary door in the wall and once I caught her trying to open the window. When I asked her what she was doing, she said she was going to the sales!

One thing that amazes me is that she never hurts herself. You would think she might fall over or hit her head or something, and that scares me. But somehow she always seems to be all right. I've found her asleep in all sorts of strange places in the house after sleepwalking.

Often while she is sleepwalking she says things. Sometimes it is meaningless, but I've noticed that she often seems to be seeing angels. One time, she told me not to sit on the chair because the angel was sitting there. Another time, she kept telling me to look at the angels and saying how beautiful they were. She doesn't remember any of this when she wakes up, so I can't ask her to tell me what they look like.

One time, she was asleep at the top of the stairs and I asked her what she was doing there. She was still half-asleep and said that the angel had stopped her from going down the stairs. Once I even found her in the car, but thankfully she didn't have the keys, so she hadn't managed to start it up. She said that the angel had taken the keys off her. And the keys had indeed been moved from the hook over the door and put on top of the fridge, so something had happened.

The last time she was sleepwalking, I woke up and found her in the front room talking to someone I couldn't see. I asked her who she was talking to. She said the angels had brought Ellie to see her. Now Ellie was a friend of hers who died ten years ago in a car crash. My wife misses her very much.

These things could all just be in my wife's imagination, or dreams. But I found the thing with the car keys unsettling, because it seemed like what she was saying might really be true. To be honest, I don't know what to think, but it is all fascinating. It does tend to make me think that the angels are there to look after her when she is at risk.

CARL
Hawaii, USA

I was out scuba diving with some friends last year when one of our friends, Rob, hurt his leg badly on something under the water. We tried to help him, but he seemed to be sucked back under the water. We looked around for him for about ten or fifteen minutes but we'd lost sight of him. It was a desperate and terrifying moment for us. We decided to head back to shore in our boat and report it to the coast authority.

When we got back to the beach, Rob was sitting on the sand having his leg attended to by a medical attendant. When we asked him what had happened, he said he remembered being picked up by a man in a small dinghy and brought back to shore. We felt fairly sure there had been no other boats around that afternoon. I don't know how Rob was helped, but maybe it was some kind of angel who arrived in his hour of need.

ERIC, 72
Manchester, England

I saw an angel this winter. I was ill with pneumonia—
they call it "the old person's friend," because if you're too
frail, it's not such a bad way to die. It takes a lot of people
in the winter. I was at home, being looked after by my
daughter Alice. She had been sitting with me in the evening, and she was sleeping downstairs in the front room,
because I'd been so ill she was worried about me.

I was lying on my back and feeling bad. I really needed
to sleep and I was struggling to breathe because my lungs
were so congested. I started falling asleep and at the same
time I could feel my heart fluttering and jumping. Then
I saw the angel. He was quite faint but I could see him
clearly, standing beside the bed. He was just watching,
though he looked concerned. It was like the look people
give you in the hospital when they're not sure what to
say.

It was a real struggle, but I made myself sit up and shout
for Alice, then I fell down on the bed. It turned out I'd had
a little stroke—nothing really serious in that I got over it.
I might have more strokes in the future, but don't worry—
I'll be around for a while yet.

JAMES
Aran, Scotland

We had a bad blizzard a couple of winters ago. There was
a very heavy snowfall and strong winds. Part of the tiling
on our roof came off overnight, and the next morning I

set about trying to mend it despite the weather, because it would be letting water into the house.

I was up the ladder when it started to feel as if someone was shaking it at the bottom. I couldn't see very well because of the snow falling, so I went back down the ladder to see what was the matter. I was suddenly dragged with some force across the path, away from the ladder, and at about the same time a very heavy amount of snow fell off the roof, taking half the roof with it. I would almost certainly have been badly injured or killed if I had been at the top of the ladder. I don't know who or what pulled me away, but I like to think it was my guardian angel looking out for me.

ANGELA, 23
London, England

I've got an angel who looks after me on the train on my way to work. I have to get a train at 7:55 in the morning to get to my office on time, although I sometimes get the 8:10 if I've had a bit of trouble getting up. It doesn't matter which one I take; it's always packed and I almost never get a seat. I don't mind too much, unless it's really hot, because the journey only takes about twenty minutes and I'm quite happy listening to my Walkman.

The only really unpleasant thing about it, apart from all the people with bad breath or too much perfume on, is that I often seem to get jammed up against horrible men. They hardly ever say anything, but they're always trying to look down my top or get much closer to me than they need to. I don't know why some men do that. Do they really think they're going to get a date by being horrible and intimidating? Anyway, I don't have to worry about it anymore, because there's an angel who watches out for me. I've never actually seen him, although I think I caught a glimpse of him once, but I've felt him and I've heard him.

The first time he helped me I was on the train and there was a man standing in front of me who actually did start saying stuff to me—about how I looked, how I was dressed. It was really horrible and I couldn't get away because it was so crowded. Nobody else was taking any notice; they probably couldn't hear him, but I bet that they wouldn't have helped even if they could have. Normally I'd have been listening to the radio but the batteries had run down. I was trying to ignore him, but I was getting more and more upset when I felt a hand on my shoulder.

Under the circumstances I'm amazed that I didn't completely freak out, but it immediately felt so comforting that I didn't even think of turning round and seeing who it was. At the same time, I heard a lovely, deep soft voice say, "Don't worry, Angela. I'll deal with this." His voice came from about a foot above me, and I'm five foot six, so he must have been pretty tall. The man who was talking at me didn't seem to have noticed anything until my angel said, "I don't think the lady's interested in anything you've got to say." And although his voice sounded just as soft and deep and lovely to me, he must have looked scary or something, because the man in front of me went white and shut up straight away.

When the train stopped, the door was behind me and I got stuck getting off, so I didn't see who had helped me out. I didn't realize then that he was an angel; I just thought it was somebody being kind. But then it happened again the next week. Someone was staring at me and I felt the angel's hand—it's very warm and heavy—and heard his voice again saying exactly the same thing, that I shouldn't worry and he'd deal with it. He did, and I looked for him and couldn't find him. This time, though, it did occur to me to wonder how someone I'd never even seen knew my name. After it had happened another few times, I realized that I was never going to get to see him and, in a way, I'm almost glad because he could be quite frightening, going by the reaction he gets. The men all look terrified when he speaks to them. I don't think I'd see that side of him, though; I think I'd just see a beautiful angel with big hands and a deep, gentle voice. Don't get me wrong, it's not like I expect him to be there. I don't want to take advantage, but I always feel really safe knowing that he probably will be.

MESSENGER ANGELS

In this section, I have included a variety of incidents in which the main action of the angels was to carry a message to a person. In some cases, the message seems to be from someone far away. In other cases, it is from someone who has died. The latter might seem to be something that belongs in a book about ghosts, and I excluded some stories on the basis that they were solely about the spirits of the deceased. But in other cases, the teller of the story believed that he or she had been brought a message by an angel, and this role of angel as intermediary is one that seems to be common enough to include here.

Finally, there are accounts of messages that seem to be divine. The most ancient role of angels was as go-betweens between heaven and earth. As beings who can exist in either realm, they are the chosen messengers of God. The accounts here that fall into this category come from people of different religions, though in each case they have a firm faith in their god. I sometimes wonder if these cases are actually situations in which the angels have chosen to intervene of their own accord. This is a theological question, and a difficult one to answer. What-ever the explanation, such messages have had a profound effect in people's lives, and as such are extremely interest-ing and valuable.

SAM, 53
Colorado, USA

I used to be a heavy drug user. I would take anything and everything, but things had got to a bad state when I started doing heroin regularly. That's the point where I had given up the idea of any kind of meaning and purpose in life, and was prepared to totally give up my life to the drug. And it takes over your whole life. You're getting the money to-gether for a fix, or out of your head on the drug, or getting over it and getting ready to find some more. Nothing else matters.

I actually got a phone call. It sounds ridiculous, but I suppose it doesn't matter how angels communicate with you. I was in my apartment one day, with the previous night's fix wearing off. I was a mess, lying there, filthy, sur-rounded by takeout trays and mess. The phone rang and it was a man's voice I had never heard before.

He said, "Sam, look at yourself. I know you. You don't have to be like this. It's time for a change."

"Who are you?" I asked.

"It doesn't matter," he said. "I remember you up at that lake when your marriage broke up. I know you didn't want to end up like this."

That was pretty weird, because I never talked to anyone about that. In fact I'd pretty much forgotten, but after my wife walked out, I took the tent up to a lake I know up in the hills. I slept there for three days. I had nothing but water and some bread, fruit, and beans with me. I went to get away from everything and while I was there, I felt great. It seemed like even though things had fallen apart, I could start again. It seemed like life was full of possibilities. It was the perfect thing to remind me of, because it was a time in my life when, even though things weren't great, I was coping and being positive. That feeling had gradually slipped away, and I had gotten more and more negative over the years until I'd forgotten all about it.

"How do you know about that?" I asked.

"Do you need to ask?" he said. And that was it; the line went dead.

I actually got fixed up that night. But even while I was doing it, I felt more and more disgusted with myself. I hadn't thought about the time at the lake in years, but now it came back to me and I could see for myself that I didn't need to be like this.

The day after that, I checked into rehab. It was really difficult, but I got myself clean and I've stayed that way ever since. It's not easy. I don't feel great every day. But there are some days when I get that feeling back that I had at the lake—that I can do anything and the world is a wonderful place. It's worth being off the drugs just to feel like that now and then. I don't even drink coffee or beer now; it's just water and herb tea. I miss the stimulants, but I know that they weren't good for me because I never knew when to stop. I needed to be told and thankfully someone did it for me.

HESTER, 72
Mississippi, USA

My mother died when I was ten. She had a growth in her stomach and the doctors couldn't do anything about it. Before that, my father hadn't had much to do with us children. I had two sisters and a brother, all younger than me. He used to drink and gamble and sometimes he'd stay away for days at a time. But when my mother died he was left with the four of us, which must have been a shock.

He changed completely. He used to get up early to make us breakfast and get us ready for school, then he'd work all day. I'd look after the other three after school until he came home. Then he'd make us food, get us bathed, and go on working right through until I went to bed—washing clothes, chopping wood, whatever was needed. He gave up drinking and worked so hard looking after us. He even used to take us to church on Sundays, and I'd never in my life seen him in church before that.

When I was eighteen, I got married and he gave me away. The night before, we stayed up talking and he told me that the night after my mother died, he had met an angel. It came into his room and told him that his wife wanted him to promise to look after us. She hadn't been

able to say this before she died. He said the angel was like
a woman, but that she was shining with light. He knew
she was an angel right away. He had promised and had
done everything he could. I told him then what I truly
believed, that no one could have done it better.

He died in 1982, and he lived to see us all grow up and
get married. He ended up with ten beautiful grandchildren and I think he was a happy man in his life. I remember him and my mother with great love and picture them
together in heaven.

KAREN, 38
Michigan, USA

I have a good friend, Alice, who lives in the country. She
has an old farmhouse with some land around it. She lives
there with her husband, but he is often away traveling.
She keeps some animals—a couple sheep, a pig, a goat,
and a bunch of geese, as well as all the cats. It's a lovely
place.

One morning, just before dawn, I woke up and there
was an angel standing at the bottom of my bed. She was
tall, dressed in white, and very vivid in the half-light.
She just said, "Alice needs you," and then she was gone.
I closed my eyes and shook my head, but she didn't come
back. I thought it must be a dream, and for a moment I
started going back to sleep. But then I thought to myself, what if that was a real angel, and Alice really is in
trouble?

Feeling a little ridiculous, I got up, threw some clothes
on, and got into the car. I drove the twenty miles out to

Alice's place. When I got there, it was about six in the morning and I was totally awake as it was quite cold. I wondered what to do—if I should go in or not. In the end, I figured that the worst that could happen was that Alice would think I was crazy. So I went into the yard and started walking to the house.

Then I heard Alice shouting somewhere. The animals were all wandering around aimlessly and I had to get round them to find where she was. Around the back of the house there was a huge hole in the ground, and when I got there, I saw Alice at the bottom, lying down, and looking kind of bedraggled and muddy. "Karen," she said. "How did you know I was here?" I told her I just had a funny feeling about her and came to check.

What had happened was that Ted, her husband, had been digging the foundations for a new barn the week before. He had this crazy idea of building one of those real old New England-style barns; he even had all the timber ready in the old barn. While Alice was feeding the geese, the goat had been acting up, and while she was trying to calm him down, she had gotten too close to the edge. The earth had crumbled away and she had fallen in. "Like a bear in a trap," she said. She'd fractured her ankle in the fall, too, so she was in a lot of pain.

I managed to get her out by tying a rope to a nearby tree and helping her haul herself out. The hole wasn't that deep, but with her ankle all busted up, she couldn't have done it by herself. She'd been there since sundown the night before, so she was really cold and thirsty. I managed to get her fed and warm, and then I drove her to the hospital. I helped her out at the farm for a couple of days until Ted got back, and then he had to stay around while she recovered. He even managed to build his barn while he was helping look after her.

Alice was really grateful to me for coming along, but I never told her that it was more than just a hunch that got me there.

Ruth, 40
Michigan, USA

I used to be in a religious cult. I dropped out of college and joined up. I won't tell you which one, because I'd rather not, but it was the usual thing—a charismatic man we called Leader. We gave up all our possessions and gave him all our money. We had to break off all previous friendships and relationships, even family.

It's hard to understand now, but I was a bit unbalanced while I was at college. It appealed to something puritanical in me, to simplify everything that way and devote myself to God. And while the Leader was making money off of us, we did genuinely do some good things, too. We used to run a homeless shelter in the city and gave free meals to the poor and all that. I could feel good about it at the time.

But after a year or two, I was becoming more aware of the fact that the Leader was rich in spite of preaching self-denial, and that sometimes the instructions he gave followers to break off relationships were the cause of suffering. There was a mother who was always trying to come to the shelter to track down her son, who had joined the cult. So the Leader sent him to another city, and we were instructed to tell her nothing. The poor woman was distraught, and I couldn't see why it would be so terrible for her to know where he was. I never got along with my family that well, so for me that was no great hardship, but I could see that it was for others.

Around the time that the woman was coming into the shelter, crying her eyes out, I had a dream. An angel came to me. It was huge, white, with wings and a stern face. It was exactly like the angels you see in religious paintings, like the one telling Mary that she was to be the mother of God. I was frightened in the dream and hid my face.

The angel spoke to me. I asked it if the Leader had told it to come. It said that it had never spoken to the Leader and that he was further from God than I was. It looked angry when it said this, and I realized that of course the angel came from God, so all earthly leaders were nothing compared to that. That was all that the angel said, but it stayed standing over me for a long time.

When I woke up, I thought for a long time about the angel, and about what it had wanted to tell me. I didn't feel that I was especially close to God. If anything, that was why I had felt I should join the cult. But if the Leader was further from God than me, that either meant that I was close to God or that the Leader was far from God. Given everything that I knew, the latter seemed to me to be the better interpretation. The angel was warning me that I was following a man who was not close to God.

I left the cult. It was incredibly difficult to do. It meant leaving behind a new group of friends, many of whom were dear to me. There was a lot of pressure put on me by the Leader and his friends. I was told that if I left, I could never come back, that I would never see my friends again, that God wanted me to stay, and so on. I'm not sure I'd have been brave enough to go if I hadn't had the image of that angel in my mind. And also, the way I was treated at this time made it very clear that the Leader was not a good man, and that he was self-regarding and cruel. But nonetheless I found it hard to leave it all behind because it was the only certain thing in my life.

Once I left, I had to start my life over again. My old friends were understandably distant with me and my family still treated me as though I was crazy. But I managed to find new people, and work, and to gradually build something like a normal life. Later, I met up with a few others who had been brave enough to leave the cult, and that helped a lot because they were the only people I could really talk to and laugh with about it. I think it was when I started to be able to laugh about it that I really started to recover and leave it behind.

To meet me now, you would never know that I used to be in the cult. I am married to a good man and we have three lovely children. I get along with my family now, to a degree, and I live a normal life.

When I think about the angel, I think there are two possibilities. One is that it was a real angel that came to me with a message about where my life was going. That's my real belief, because it was so remarkable and vivid. But the other possibility is that it was something from my subconscious mind. Maybe I projected an angel to tell me the things that I was subconsciously starting to realize. I'm not sure—my husband thinks that it was probably my subconscious; I think it was probably an angel. But even if it wasn't a real angel, it was a moment that had a profound impact on my life, because at the time I listened to the angel and took its words as being a message from God.

HELEN
California, USA

About four years ago, I had a miscarriage. I was so upset about it and the depression that followed caused me to eventually split from my boyfriend. I sank even deeper into depression and eventually quit my job because I felt I just couldn't cope with anything anymore.

I spent months just sitting around my apartment doing nothing. I was gaining weight and beginning to look terrible. A friend gave me a puppy, saying it would help to get me out and about a bit more. I started going jogging round the park with Sidney, my little dog, chasing at my heels. One day as I was walking, an old woman came up to me and said, "It doesn't have to be like this, you know. You are loved."

I took her to mean that God loved me and that I needed to get my life back on track. I went to the hair salon and got a hair makeover and bought some new, smarter clothes. I began applying for jobs and within three months got a great job in public relations. It was a real career that I could concentrate on.

Now, every time I feel a bit down, I remember the words of the old woman: "You are loved, you know." It really helps.

Don, 46
Pennsylvania, USA

I have always been faithful to my wife, but once I nearly strayed. There was a woman I worked with, Sara, who I had always kind of flirted with. She moved away but I stayed in touch. Since she worked in the same industry as me, that gave us an excuse.

I went away to a conference in Chicago. I'd already made an excuse to my wife about how I wouldn't make it back on Sunday night, as there was a late meeting I had to go to. I'd said I'd be staying at a motel somewhere and coming back the next day. But actually, my last meeting was at noon and I was driving down to see Sara. I'd arranged it with her on the phone and she'd made it pretty clear that I could stay with her. I might be making assumptions there, but I'm pretty sure that if I'd gone to see her, something would have happened. I felt guilty about going to see her, but also excited.

There's nothing wrong with my wife or with my marriage. I think that every now and then you go through a period when you panic about where you are in life, and worry about growing old without doing everything you possibly can. It's not a very healthy way of thinking, but when you go through one of those periods, you are at your weakest. I'd managed to justify to myself what I was doing by thinking about all the difficult things about my marriage and my wife, but there was no excuse, really.

What happened was I picked up a hitchhiker. He was a man of about my age, with gray eyes. He turned out to be going where I was going. He started talking to me about where I came from, whether or not I was married and all that. He was particularly interested to hear about my wife and children. He told me that he'd been married once, but had made some terrible mistakes and thrown it away, and that he regretted it every day. You can imagine that that wasn't I wanted to hear at that moment. But anyway, I asked him about it, and he told me a bit about how he'd undervalued his wife and argued with her, and how in the end she had thrown him out.

We were quiet for a few miles, then he asked me about where I was staying that night. I said I hadn't decided yet and he said that was good—better to leave it until I had to decide. Then he told me that I could drop him where we were. It was kind of the middle of nowhere, but he said he could cut across the fields to where he was going.

Just as he got out, he thanked me for the ride and turned back to look straight at me. He said, "Wherever you go tonight, I hope you will think very hard about the consequences." I thanked him but didn't ask him what he was saying, because I knew exactly what he meant. I hadn't told him anything about Sara but he knew. What he'd already said had been enough to give me pause for thought, but this was as though he felt he hadn't been direct enough and maybe he was right.

I got to Sara's town and stopped at a restaurant to think. Then I drove up the street to a motel. I was only a mile or two from her house, but I called to say I was stuck miles away with a flat tire. She said it was a shame, maybe another time, but we both knew there probably wouldn't be another time.

I went to a bar and got drunk and slept badly, then got up early and drove home. I was truly relieved to see my wife and to be able to look her in the eye. I think it would have been a big mistake if I had gone to see Sara, so for whatever reason I'm grateful that the hitchhiker talked to me in the way he did. I'm inclined to think he was an angel, because he just knew a bit too much and happened to come into my life at exactly the right time. It's too much of a chance for that to happen, so I'm thankful he was there.

CARRIE
Sydney, Australia

A few years ago, my husband and I were looking for a house to buy. I had been told shortly after we married that I almost certainly couldn't have children. When we looked at the house where we now live, it felt really warm and homey and I loved it.

I could hear the sound of children playing next door and everything felt just right. The next-door neighbor, an elderly lady, came out and told us that we would be very happy there and that it was a good place to bring up children. I didn't want to tell her that I couldn't have children, but she was very nice and I did feel that we would be happy there.

We bought the house and moved in. The same week we moved in, I found out I was pregnant. It was like a miracle. I went next door to thank the lady for telling us to buy the house and see if she needed any shopping done, things like that. As I was knocking at the door, a man who was passing told me that the lady who used to live there had died six months ago and the house had been empty since. He also told me that no children had lived there for over forty-five years.

Whoever it was who persuaded us to buy the house, they definitely were looking after us. I'm now pregnant with my second child—a double miracle—and I can't help but think that an angel has blessed us.

ALICE, 40
Belfast, Northern Ireland

I always worry about my children when they are away from home. I have three between eighteen and twenty-five, and still I worry that I can't be there to look after them. It's silly, I suppose, but that's what it's like being a parent.

I split up with their father when the youngest was eight. I left them behind and moved ten miles away to live with friends. It was a terribly difficult decision to make. My husband and I were both very unhappy and depressed being together and we simply didn't want to stay together. He was drinking too much and I was on sleeping pills as I couldn't sleep from anxiety. In the end, I was the one that went. He was in a better position to look after them than me. I knew that logically, but still found it a horrible wrench. I saw them as often as I possibly could and kept pretty good relationships with them. It took the eldest a long time to understand or forgive me. But in the end I think they were all okay about it and now I speak to them all regularly.

A few weeks ago, I had a dream where an angel came to me in my room and told me to call Duncan, my youngest boy. I woke up early and called him. It turned out that he had had an accident. He had got very drunk with friends and tried to climb over a wall to get into a club. He had fallen badly on his head and been knocked out. When he woke up, he just went home and went to bed to sleep it off. He was still slurring his words.

I was furious at him for not going to the hospital. I made him promise me to go immediately for a check-up. I know something about concussions and I thought that if he was slurring his words, he was concussed and needed to be checked out. You can do yourself bad damage with a head injury and not realize how bad it is.

He was a bit embarrassed about it and didn't want to make a fuss, as it was his fault. But he promised me to go in a taxi for a check-up. They ended up keeping him in overnight for observation, they were so worried about the state of him when he arrived.

He was fine in the end, but I can't know what might have happened if he hadn't gone to the hospital. I shudder to think about it. I can't believe an angel would have come to me if he or she hadn't felt that he needed my help. I don't clearly remember the angel's face. I just remember the light and a feeling of great calm and serenity while we were talking.

Jane, 36
Cape Town, South Africa

I was going to get married when I was twenty, to a man called Michael. The day of the wedding, I was at home getting my hair and face made up, and about to get into my dress to set off for the church. I was sitting on my own in my room, in a bathrobe with curling tongs in my hair, when I looked up and found the room was shining, and there were three angels standing there looking at me. They just stood and looked at me and reached out their hands. Then there was a bang at the door and my sister pushed in, and they disappeared. I had no idea what was going on.

About five minutes later, there was a phone call. My father came in and told me there had been a car crash, and Michael had been in it. I was really shocked and immediately connected it to the angels. My father was telling me that Michael was probably fine and we might even be able to go ahead with the wedding, but I knew it was something more than that—because why else had the angels been there?

We had to go to the hospital, and as soon as we got there, Michael's mother came out crying. She had gotten there first and been told that there was nothing they could do. He'd died from loss of blood soon after being admitted, and they hadn't been able to resuscitate him.

It was a terrible time. I felt so cheated and miserable and bad. Everyone tried to help me afterward, but I pushed them all away. I spent the next week hiding in my room and I got some sleeping pills from the doctor so I could sleep. I told him they didn't work and got the dosage increased. After that, I was in a daze. I could barely look after myself, but I wouldn't talk to anyone about it, not even Michael's mother. The angels came several times in my dreams but I wouldn't talk to them. I used to say, "Why didn't you stop it happening?" and they'd look sad and disappear.

Finally, one morning I woke up very early—the middle of the night, really—and they were all there again. The one in the middle said, "When Michael died, he was sorry he couldn't be with you again and we're sorry we couldn't stop it. But other people need you now. Michael wouldn't want you to throw your life away." And then they went away again. I wanted them to tell me more about Michael and where he was now, but they wouldn't. They just went.

It sounds strange, but that's exactly how I remember it. Even though I was a bit dazed with the pills, I can remember their faces and the way he spoke absolutely clearly. They were just like people in simple clothes but you could tell they were angels from their faces and their eyes.

I got up that day and went out. I went to see Michael's mother. When I got there, she just started crying and holding onto me, and I realized that she had been going through a terrible time, too. I realized how selfish I was being. I still felt terrible and sad, but I saw that there were other people going through this too, and that we could help each other.

I had a hard time stopping the sleeping pills, but I forced myself to go through it. It's not like I stopped being sad overnight, but I tried harder to reach out to other people as well. Really, it took me years to get over it fully, but it was that day that I made the first small step. I didn't date anyone again for years, and it was ten years before I ever married. But I'm here now with the twins and with a happy marriage. There's still a part of my heart that misses Michael all the time, and every now and then I go to see his mother to talk. We were together from when we were teenagers so I knew them a long time. It wasn't just a little romance. But you can move on in life, and sometimes the only way to respect the dead is to do just that.

I think those angels were there to look after me, or to look after Michael, or both. I don't know if they brought me a message from Michael, or if, having not talked to me to start with, they finally felt they had to intervene themselves. But either way, they did me a good turn.

SAMANTHA
South Carolina, USA

When my daughter goes to work she usually leaves my grandson Dylan with me and I take care of him for the day. On this particular day, she decided to take the day off and we were going to drive together to see my mom and dad, who had only seen their great-grandson once in his six-month life.

I was driving and my daughter was looking out of the window and dozing. We had the radio on and it was a lovely day. Dylan had fallen asleep in his car seat in the back. As we drove down the highway, there was an announcement on the radio that our exit, fifty-two, was closed and cars should take exit fifty-one before it. We were nearly at fifty-one so it was good to be forewarned.

I did as the radio suggested and left the highway at fifty-one. As we drove up the exit ramp, my daughter asked where I was going. I said that I was following the instructions on the radio. She looked puzzled and said the radio had only been playing music and there had been no announcement. Well, I knew what I heard, so I just kept going. We drove through the residential streets to get back up to exit fifty-two. As we got closer, we heard an enormous crash and saw smoke beginning to rise from where exit fifty-two was. Just after this, we saw police cars and an ambulance racing there with sirens sounding loudly and flashing lights.

The funny thing is that the accident happened after we left the highway, not before, and my daughter still swears that she didn't hear that announcement on the radio. Maybe some kind of angel forewarned us of possible danger ahead and kept us all safely away.

FRANK, 36
Paris, France

This happened twelve years ago. I lived in Frankfurt then with my wife Ella. She was a model, quite successful in Germany. I was working for a television company on a freelance basis. Ella came home one day and told me that she had been offered a chance to go work in Tokyo for a year at a modeling agency. It was a great surprise to us both.

My initial reaction was to be pleased for her, but then I realized how difficult it would be for us to be separated for a year. We had only been together for a year or two and I didn't want to be apart from her. But to her it was all very simple. I should come with her. She would be well paid so it wouldn't matter if I couldn't immediately find work. She was expecting me to give everything up and go to Tokyo, with no idea of the language or what to do when I got there.

I understood that she wanted to go, but I suppose my pride was hurt by the idea that I should just run after her like that. So I said no, I would have to stay in Frankfurt and wait for her. She was disappointed but said she understood. And that was how we left it. She was to leave in a week; I was going to stay there.

But over the next day or two I realized that things weren't right. We started to argue over silly things. She was very cold to me, and I got it into my head that she was preparing herself to split up with me—as though she didn't want the burden of having a husband far away and would rather go to Tokyo as a single person. Subconsciously I thought she was trying to engineer a situation where she could leave me behind completely. I reacted to this by being alternately angry and upset, so I didn't do much to win her over. It seemed so unfair that our whole life should fall apart over this one thing. I felt that even if we didn't split up now, she would fall in love with being in a new place as soon as she got there and forget all about me.

One night, three days before she was due to leave, we had a row and I went out for a long walk. I walked along the river, through the park, and then across the old bridge into Sachsen-Hausen. This is the old part of Frankfurt, one of the few places that survived the war without too much damage. There are old cobbled streets and alleys. It was early evening in October and it had become quite misty, so the streets looked very intriguing, with the lights starting to glow gently through the mist. I was looking for a bar to go to.

In one alley, I found myself walking next to an old man with a white beard. He asked if I was looking for a bar and I said yes. Then he told me to listen carefully, and he started talking as though he knew all about me. He told me that I had an opportunity to leave for a new life with someone and that that someone wanted me with them. He said that I could stay if I really didn't want to be with her, but that if I stayed out of fear, it would be something I would regret.

I was amazed that he seemed to know so much. I suggested he come for a drink with me and he said yes. So I led him down the stairs into one of the underground beer halls. But when I looked back he wasn't there behind me. I went back outside and there was no sign of him.

I spent the evening thinking about what he had said. I realized that I was scared of leaving everything behind and going to a new place, and that was why I was refusing to go. It was partly my pride, but partly fear. And I did love my wife, so why wouldn't I want to be with her? But did she really want me? I couldn't be sure. The man hadn't told me that; he had only advised me about how I felt.

I went home and Ella was angry at me for being out all night. Summoning my courage, I told her I wanted to go with her after all. She just started crying and hugged me. She told me that she had been scared that I didn't want her anymore, and had thought that me not wanting to go was a sign of this. She had thought it was me being cold and trying to break things off. She told me that she didn't care about Tokyo and she'd stay if I really wanted her. I was crying too now, but I told her not to be stupid—we had to take the risk and go.

That is what we did: we went together. As soon as I arrived, I knew we were doing the right thing. It was just such an amazing, bizarre place, and we loved it straight away. I did have trouble finding work, but I managed to get some teaching work after a while (teaching American English, oddly enough), and my wife was doing well in her job. She used to be tremendously busy, so I had a lot of time to explore this fascinating place. But I was always there for her when she got home. And then I got lucky and found a better job, and we ended up staying four years before we moved away. Since then we've lived in a couple of other places, too. We're not scared of leaving everything behind because we have each other, and we always have good friends we can go back and visit.

The angel, if that's what he was, did something very important for me. We were in a stupid situation where we both thought that the other was trying to pull away, so we were both being cold and letting our relationship fall apart. By making me think about how I really felt, the angel also made me realize that I needed to know how Ella felt. If I hadn't been told to think about how I really felt, I easily could have ended up ten years later regretting losing the true love of my life. But instead, here we are still together, so much stronger for everything we have gone through.

ALBERT, 46
Bruges, Belgium

After my wife died, I was in a terrible situation. She was only forty when she died of breast cancer. I loved her from the first day I met her. She was such a lovely woman, very composed, intelligent, and beautiful. I always felt that she had made me into a better person and I found it extremely hard to cope with her loss.

She was diagnosed with cancer, and then almost immediately we were told that it had spread and that they might not be able to heal her. She deteriorated very fast, and whatever we did, we knew she wasn't going to make it. When she died, I felt completely numb and empty. I went through the motions but I felt like my life was over.

I started having dreams where an angel came and brought me messages from my wife. The angel would be there standing by my bed when I woke up. He'd tell me that my wife missed me and that she loved me. Then he'd disappear and I'd wake up properly. Another time, he told me that my wife said I had to get on with life and to stop moping over her. He said that she said she couldn't relax with me moping around down here. That's almost funny, because it sounds so exactly like something she would have said to me when she was still alive.

One morning the same thing happened, and the angel told me that she said to remember the good times and to always remember that she loved me. I managed to speak this time and ask the angel why she couldn't come to see me herself. "She can't, but I can," he said. Saying that, there was a great sense of weariness and sorrow on his face. I told him to tell her that I loved her too and that of course I wouldn't forget her. Then he was gone again. After that I didn't see him again. Often I would dream about him or I would sense my wife there in the room with me, but not be able to see her when I looked.

Whether or not an angel was bringing those messages, I started to realize that what I was hearing was the truth. We hadn't really found the way to talk about how it would be after she died when she was still with me. We were too focused on trying to enjoy the time we had left and it all happened so fast. However, I'm sure that my wife would have wanted me to go on with life and not to mope around. But also she would have wanted me to remember her. There's not a day when I don't remember her, or put aside a little time to talk to her in my mind—to talk about some little thing I remember from when she was alive. I'm still sad she died, of course, but I do try to live my life in a way that does justice to her memory.

SALLY, 43
Sydney, Australia

I have three children, but I should have had four. The third time I was pregnant, something went wrong. I was nearly six months pregnant when the baby died inside me. "No reason," they said, "Occasionally it happens. You were just unlucky. It's not your fault." But of course they would say that. They didn't want me to feel guilty and ruin my life, but somehow I felt I must be to blame for what happened.

One day the baby was kicking and wriggling inside me; the next there was nothing. I had to shout at my husband to make him believe there was something wrong, but even before they told me at the hospital, I knew it was hopeless. I knew enough to let myself go limp, to just do whatever they told me to do for the next few hours. The terrible thing is that you have to give birth knowing that there is no life there. It was ten times harder than any of my other three. I don't really want to tell you all the details, but it was bad.

Afterward they dressed him in some clothes I had brought and took some photographs for me. My husband and I reacted very differently. I wanted to hold the baby and to keep the pictures to look at. He held the baby but I could see he only did it for my sake, and he didn't really want to look at the pictures. I understand now that he just reacted his own way. For a man, a baby isn't really real until it is put into their arms kicking and screaming, but for a woman it has been there inside you. You have to mourn it the same as if it had been a living child.

Afterward I withdrew from my husband. I had to look after the two elder children, and I just became completely self-absorbed, wrapped up in my own grief. I was still angry at my husband for not reacting the same as me. For instance, he suggested that we could have another child, as though just doing that would make it all right somehow. After a few weeks of this, things were bad. He felt shut out, as though I wouldn't let him help with anything and wouldn't turn to him for comfort in those difficult times. I also realize now that I failed to see how much he was hurting too.

One night I had a kind of dream, or maybe it was more of a vision. It didn't seem at all like a dream because it was far too vivid and clear. An angel came and took me by the hand. She was dressed in white and gave off a strong light as she walked. She was very warm to the touch. She held my hand and took me for a walk. She didn't say a single word. She took me to a park, a bit like the park where we played with the children, but much larger, with huge hills and a big playground. The whole playground was full of children playing and running around happily. Somehow I understood that these were children that had died but that were carrying on a happy life elsewhere.

Then she led me on past the playground and out through a gate that led to a beach. We live miles from the sea, so this was nothing like anywhere I knew. It was a lovely calm sea, with white sand and turquoise water. We took off our shoes and walked down the sand in our bare feet. And down by the water's edge there was one tiny little baby playing by himself. It was clearly my son who had died. But he was a little older, a tiny baby sitting up, rather than how he had been when I gave birth to him.

He was happy and smiling and dangling his toes in the water. He looked up and smiled when he saw me, and put his arms out. I picked him up and held him against my heart, and he made these lovely little noises, the noises real babies make. Then I put him down and he went on playing in the edge of the water and I felt a great sense of calm. The angel motioned me to come away with her, and we walked away along a straight sandy path, and then I woke up.

It was dawn, with not much light in the room, and with that very clear vision in my mind, I just started crying and crying. I let out all the grief that I had bottled up. And my husband said nothing, but he just came and held me against him while I cried.

I think that the angel was letting me know that there are realms beyond our understanding where people live after death in many different ways. I don't know if she really took me to meet him where he was, or if she was just showing me that his soul was real and still there. And also she was helping me to realize that I was feeling sorry for myself rather than for my lost child. He couldn't have known any different from what he experienced, so for him death was not a tragedy, whereas for me it was a tragedy because I never got to see him alive.

Finally the angel gave me a last chance to say goodbye to my son in my heart and I tried to take that. As long as I could remember the sight of his little face on that beach, I held it close to me and sent him my love. I came to realize I was being unfair to my husband. We were both dealing with the same thing in our own ways, and we needed more than anything to give each other support. I did much better after that and talked to him about how he was feeling as well as how I was feeling. I realized how much he had been holding in his grief, because he knew that no matter how bad he felt, his grief couldn't quite be the same as the grief I felt as a mother at having a part of me die. But nonetheless he was devastated too.

It took me a year to come round to wanting another child, but I'm so glad we did. She's called Rose and she is a wonderful little thing, full of joy and life (and tears and tantrums of course, but it all works out in the end). Of course I still keep the photos the hospital gave me and look at them sometimes, and I feel helpless and sad. But then I put them away and get on with loving my husband and our three lovely children.

Antonia, 55
Glasgow, Scotland

My son and daughter-in-law were on holiday with their two children when the tsunami came on Boxing Day, 2004. They were in Phuket, so could easily have been killed.

I was awakened by an angel who told me that my family was okay, but that they couldn't talk to me yet. It was a woman standing right there by my bed, shaking me awake and telling me that. And then she was gone. I didn't even know what had happened. I was completely confused until I got a call from my sister, who sounded like she'd been crying. She asked if I'd seen the news, which I hadn't. She told me that there had been a tsunami and that a lot of people had been killed.

So of course I spent the day watching the television in mounting horror. I tried calling my son but of course all the lines were dead, and I guessed that he would have the same trouble. I got a lot of calls from close friends wanting to know if I had heard from my son and daughter-in-law. I kept saying I hadn't, but I was sure they were all right. Everyone was amazed at how calm I was, but I was sure that I had been lucky enough to get a message from an angel. I was confident that they hadn't been hurt.

Finally, at about midnight, I got a quick call from my son on a borrowed mobile. They had been really lucky. The hotel they were staying at was on the beach, and they had been sleeping in a beach hut only an hour before the waves came. But they were up early and happened to be lucky in that people there saw the early signs of the coming storm and recognized them, and started to run for high ground, shouting at everyone to follow them. A lot of people got away because of that, my family included. The biggest waves stopped about fifty feet away from where they had run to. Their things were ruined, including their phones, but that is nothing compared to surviving a disaster like that. They saw a lot of terrible things, of course, and did their best to help with the clean up. It was a terrible tragedy for so many people, but I was thankful that my own loved ones were not hurt.

Anja
Malmo, Sweden

I was a single mother. I won't tell you the whole story, but when my daughter Mina was three, I went through a time when I was quite depressed. I used to take Mina to the playground and do the shopping, but other than that, I didn't really interact with anyone. It is very difficult being at home all the time when you have been used to living a normal life and going out with people.

You start to feel quite hopeless and as a result you lose confidence. Even when my mother looked after Mina for an evening or an afternoon, I used to just go home and sit there. I enjoyed the peace of being on my own for a while, but I was too scared to go out and actually do anything different.

My aunt made a suggestion to me, which I thought was a terrible idea. She suggested I should work as a childminder, or nanny. I asked her what she was talking about—here I was exhausted from looking after one child, how could I take on more? But then I got to thinking about it more, and I thought that just maybe this was something I could try that would at least be a bit different. So I put out some advertisements in the local baby clothes shops and in the cafés. I waited, but I only got one reply. They were a young couple who both worked.

I had looked into all the rules and had made sure that my home was prepared for their visit. It was made even more child-friendly, and a room next to the kitchen had been cleared to be the main room I would use for doing the work. The child was only nine months old, but the mother wanted to go back to work full time. Her mother helped her two days a week but they needed someone for the other three. They were happy to give me the job. We arranged that we would start the following Monday for a trial of half a day, following up with the full schedule the week after if it went well. You could see that the mother was nervous about leaving her child with someone else, but we got on well.

That night I looked at the figures and realized that I would, by the time my allowances and tax were adjusted, hardly be better off than when I didn't work. In fact, even twice the amount of work wouldn't make that big a difference. Then I started to panic about whether or not I could cope with another child. Such a young one, too! I was only just done with nappies and bottles and all that myself, and now I was voluntarily going back to do it again.

I worried and worried that it wasn't going to work out. On Sunday, I phoned the mother and cancelled. I told her I wouldn't be able to do it after all. I didn't give any excuses; I didn't have to because I got her answering machine.

On Monday, I felt even more depressed—a kind of emptiness and resignation worse than anything I'd been through. I walked Mina around to my mother's house and went into town to do the shopping, but I really didn't feel like it. Instead I started walking around the shops in town. I went into a little art gallery that sells cheap art and framed reproductions.

There was a picture of an angel on the wall. It was a very beautiful, quite traditional, image of a winged angel dressed in white. It was unclear if it was a man or woman, but the angel was looking straight at you as you looked into the picture.

I stood there staring at the picture, and for some reason I couldn't take my eyes off it. These thoughts came into my mind as though they were from outside me. I started thinking that I was being selfish, and also that I wasn't seeing things clearly. That there was something much more important about this decision than just the money or the way I might feel inside. I looked at the angel and asked it if I had made the wrong decision. Of course I didn't get an actual message, but I had the overpowering feeling that I had done something wrong. It was like someone was taking me out of the box I had put myself into and letting me look at my life from the outside.

From there, it was very clear that I was making a narrow, ungenerous choice in life. I couldn't really afford it, but I bought the picture, took it home with me, and put it on the wall. As I walked in the door with Mina, and with the angel wrapped under my arm, the phone rang and it was the mother of the child I was supposed to look after. She was ringing to see if I was okay, as I had sounded a little strange on the phone. She wanted to reschedule a time for a trial, as she had misunderstood my message. She had thought I was just canceling the Monday rather than the whole arrangement. I arranged to do it the next day and I praised my luck that I had another chance to see what would happen.

Well, it was extremely hard work, and to start with it didn't make me that much money. It was hard looking after Mina and a little one. But soon after that I had another client, a friend of the first mother. Because I had to entertain the children, I started going out to parks and to cafés and to local children's clubs, and I started meeting other childminders and mothers. To a far greater degree than before, I started to interact with other people. Between that and the fact that I was just too busy to think about myself, I started to feel less depressed.

It wouldn't work for everyone, of course. It is such hard work but it made me really enjoy life, being around children all the time. It was good for Mina, too, as she spent time playing with the other children and teaching them what she knew. They all loved her and her social skills improved. It was clearly the right thing for me to have done, and if I had given up because of fear I would have been missing a real opportunity.

In the end, I started a nursery with a couple of the other childminders and managed to make a real business of it. So for me, there was a happy ending. To this day, I have that painting of an angel on my wall and I stand there when I have difficult decisions to make. I don't always feel that I am getting a message from outside. Sometimes I just go there out of habit. But I remember that feeling of seeing my life from the outside and that helps me to stay balanced.

Irina, 47
Moscow, Russia

One morning it was snowing very heavily; the temperature was well below zero. My mother had been ill for some time at the hospital. Whenever I could, I went to visit her, but this was a work day. I work at the local library, cataloguing new books as they come in.

I set off for work as usual. I walk—it takes about half an hour. About ten minutes away from the library, I met a man who I felt that I vaguely recognized, someone who worked in the library. He hailed me and called me over. He told me that he had just come from the library and that the heating had broken down overnight. As a result, he said, the library was closed for the day. "Are you sure?" I asked. He was very definite that it was closed and that I needn't go any farther. Then he asked if there was anything else I could do now that I was in town, and of course I thought of my mother. I told him I'd go and see my mother at the hospital—I don't know why I told him that; after all, I didn't really know him. I was just grateful that he had saved me the last bit of my journey. I remember that he smiled and seemed pleased for me.

When I arrived at the hospital, the nurse met me at the door. It turned out that my mother had become more ill overnight and they hadn't been able to get through to me on the phones. Perhaps the lines were down in the snow. I saw my mother and, even though she was unable to speak, she held my hand and looked me in the eyes. She died that morning, quite peacefully, and I was so glad that I managed to see her that one last time. I was sure that, had I gone to the library, I would have been too late, even if they had managed to call me there.

But the thing is, the library was not closed. The heating had not broken and the library was open as usual. Of course they wondered where I was, but when I explained later on—about my mother, that is—they understood.

And I never again saw the man who had diverted me on my journey. He wasn't someone who worked at the library. I'm sure, because I went looking everywhere to thank him. I'm convinced that he gave me the message because he somehow knew my mother was dying.

MARCELLO, 64
Rio de Janeiro, Brazil

An angel came to me when my brother died. He was shot in a robbery that went wrong at a supermarket. He was just in the wrong place while someone else was trying to steal money. He was fifty-two, too young to die. I was at work at the time and a strange man walked into my office. He said, "Go home now. Go to your mother." He was the sort of person you want to obey; he had that kind of aura. He didn't look particularly strange, just distinguished. Someone to respect.

So I went home and my mother seemed fine, but then there was the knock at the door and the police arrived to tell us my brother was dead. My mother pretty much collapsed, so I was glad that I was there. It was terrible for her. At seventy you think you won't outlive your children, and he was always a favorite of hers. They were very close and it was awful for her to lose him like that.

I can't say yes, that was definitely an angel. I might have passed that man in the street and not noticed him. It's not like there was a heavenly light or a thunderclap or anything like that. But I just can't think how else to explain it.

EDUARDO
Barcelona, Spain

When I was a child, there was river near our house that always dried up in the summertime. We all used to play there during the long, hot summer holidays. I remember this strange-looking African man used to walk past, followed by a white cat. They made a strange sight as they walked through the dried-up fields and riverbeds.

He always said, "Good day, Eduardo," and I always said hello back. Sometimes, if I was on my own, he would sit down and chat with me for a little while. As he talked, he would look at my palm and tell my future. He told me that when I grew up I would move to the city, have a beautiful wife and a lovely home. He predicted that I would have three children, and they would all be fortunate and go to university and become professional people. Once, he stopped by where I was playing and told me to go home immediately—my mother needed me, he said. I got to my feet and ran home.

My mother was so glad to see me. My grandmother, who was visiting, had collapsed on the floor and could not get up. I ran for the doctor, who ran back to our house with me. He diagnosed a heart attack and called an ambulance to get her to the hospital. The fact that we had acted so quickly saved my grandmother's life.

Later I remember my mother saying how fortunate it was that I came home when I did. I told her that the African man had told me that she wanted me home. She looked confused and said she didn't know any African man, except for one old family legend dating back to the 1800s. My great-great-grandfather had saved the life of a traveling African man who had been bitten by a snake. Apparently he said he would return the favor and look out for my grandfather's family.

I knew that, although that man must be long dead, he had come back to keep his promise. As for the rest of it, well, I moved to Barcelona. I have a beautiful wife and three gorgeous children, who as yet are too young for college. But they are all clever children and will make something of their lives, that's for sure.

CAREY, 34
Minnesota, USA

I often hear angels talking to me. I know that they are there around us all the time. I speak to them in my mind when I need a little help, or when I'm not sure what to do, I ask their guidance. And they answer me. Angels don't say a lot. They just tell you exactly what you need to know, nothing more or less. They are very calm and considered. I think everyone should be able to speak to the angels around them, but if you don't have the faith in them, perhaps you don't hear what they have to say.

It's not like praying. I pray too, about the big problems in life or about the terrible things that happen in the world. But it feels wrong to ask too much of God, whereas angels are there all the time and can help with even quite small problems.

I used to have a boyfriend who was very difficult to be around. He used to go into jealous rages if I spoke to another man. I remember speaking to an angel about him. I asked if I should feel sorry for him, because he obviously had problems of rejection in his life that made him worry about these things. Or should I just be angry because he didn't respect me?

The angel just said, "He is how he is; you can't change him. The question for you is: can you be happy with him?" I thought a long time about what the angel had said and realized that I had to break up with him. The angel had realized that I was putting up with abusive treatment because, deep down, I thought I could change him. But I couldn't, and it was never going be okay between us. He actually ended up marrying someone I know, and she seems to be fine with him. Every relationship works differently, and there was just something wrong between us.

My mother left home when I was small, and for a long time I didn't see her. She moved away and my father and her weren't talking. I used to speak to the angels about how I missed her, and they would tell me that she missed me too. But when I asked if I should go and find her, they would say that I should wait. Then, when I was eighteen, the answer changed—they told me to go find her. So I did and it turned out to be the best thing I ever did. It turned out that she had gone off with another man, which my father had never told me about. I don't think I could have coped with this earlier; it would have made me angry at her and angry at my father for not telling me. But when I finally did meet up with her, I was old enough that I knew the strange ways that love can work. So I could forgive her and understand what she had gone through, rather than just hating her for abandoning us. I'm so happy that she is back in my life again. The angels also told me to be careful with my father. For a whole year, I didn't tell him I had seen my mother. Then he got together with Alison, a lovely woman who made him happy, and at last I agreed with the angels it was time to tell him.

Writing them down, these all seem like small personal matters, nothing compared to the problems of the world. But they are things that have been very important in my life and that the angels have helped me understand.

ANGELS, SPIRIT GUIDES, AND GHOSTS

Exactly how angels are related to the spirits of people who have died is a problem I discussed previously. It seems unlikely that people who die become angels. The bulk of evidence is against this view, as angels seem to be quite a different kind of entity than a spirit. Nonetheless, there are many accounts of "angelic" visitations from beyond the grave, and I received a lot of accounts that could be considered to be about spirits of the deceased rather than about angels. In some cases, the conviction of the teller that a departed friend or family member became an angel was sufficiently compelling that I thought it best to include the account and allow readers to decide for themselves what to think.

I excluded those accounts that clearly seemed to be about ghosts and ghosts only; however, in a few cases, the spirits of the deceased seem to be guided back to loved ones through the intervention of an angel. In deciding which accounts to include in this section, I have tried to select a variety that covers all aspects of the topic.

ANNIE, 34
Newcastle, England

When I was a kid, I spent a lot of time being looked after by my Aunt Rosie. She wasn't really my aunt; she was an old friend of my mother's who lived a few houses up the street. She was retired, but she still used to work as a cleaner. She would work early in the morning and then later, after the factory or office was closed. As a result, she was around in the daytime, and used to look after me while my mother went to work. She did this when I was young, and then kept on doing it in the school holidays after I went to school.

Rosie died when I was ten. I wanted to go to the funeral, but everyone thought I was too young. I think my mother underestimated how strong our bond was. I still loved my mother, but I had spent so much time with Rosie, I loved her in the same kind of way. I spent the whole day crying and it took me a while even to start getting over it. Rosie was the one adult I could talk to about absolutely anything. If I asked my mum about growing up, or marriage, or what happens after you die, she wouldn't know what to say, but Rosie would always just tell me what she thought and let me make my own mind up.

When I was about thirteen, I was going through a difficult patch at school. My best friend had moved away to another school, and I was unhappy because I didn't really have any other close friends there. I felt very isolated. One night I woke up in the night and went downstairs. There was a knock at the door, and when I opened it, there was Rosie, with a woman standing behind her in the street. Rosie asked if she could come in, and I said of course she could. Then we sat down there in the front room and talked about everything that had happened to me since she died. It was lovely to see her again, and it made me feel a lot better. I don't remember what happened after that until my mother came down and found me curled up asleep on the front room floor. I couldn't really say if it was a dream or if it really happened, but I'd definitely gone downstairs in the night somehow. Maybe it was a kind of sleepwalking, but I felt like I really had seen Rosie.

This started happening regularly. It was almost like, if I really needed to talk to someone or if I was confused, Rosie would always come and have a chat with me. I used to wake up in funny places; once I was asleep halfway up the stairs. My mum even put a safety gate on my door because she thought I was sleepwalking, but it didn't stop me.

Every time Rosie came, there was the same woman with her. She arrived with her, then seemed to wait outside while Rosie talked to me, then they would leave together. Once I asked Rosie who she was. She didn't really explain, but she said that the woman helped her come to see me. I believe that the woman was an angel. I'm very grateful, because

Rosie helped me a lot through those years. I haven't seen her now for a long time, but I have a feeling that if I ever really, really needed her, she might still come and talk to me.

HOLLY, 30
Florida, USA

I met my grandmother with an angel once. She died when I was six, so I don't remember her that well, but apparently I was a favorite of hers, and I used to stay with her often. I do remember playing with her, and making houses out of cardboard boxes and pretending that cotton reels were little people living in the houses. And I remember being happy when I was with her.

About ten years ago, I was up very early and walking down on the beach. There was no one else around. Then I met two women walking the other way. They weren't old, perhaps in their forties. One looked very much like the pictures I have seen of my grandmother when she was younger.

They said hello, and I blurted out to this woman that she looked like my grandmother. She just laughed and asked if I remembered her kindly. I told her what I remembered. Then she asked me how I was, and if I was happy. I told her about my life, and how I was going to get married soon, and what I was studying and where I worked. Silly things like that, but she wanted to know.

Then she had to go. The other woman hardly spoke the whole time, but it was she that said they had to go. I asked the woman who looked like my grandmother if she really was my grandmother and she just laughed again, but kindly.

I asked her, if she wasn't my grandmother, was she an angel? She just laughed again and said no, but that maybe her friend was. And she said that maybe her friend had let her come to see me to check that I was happy. She put her hand on my shoulder and said how happy she was to see me all grown up. Then they walked off. It didn't even occur to me to walk after them—I just knew I couldn't. Later on, even I could hardly believe it had happened, but it really did.

NORMA
Oban, Scotland

My grandfather died when I was about nine years old. He hadn't been ill; he died suddenly of a heart attack in the local betting shop one Saturday afternoon. We always went over to my grandmother and granddad's house for tea on Saturdays and my grandmother would make these wonderful cakes.

They lived on top of this hill and you could see right down into the town from their front garden. I often used to go and swing on the gate, waiting for him to come home, so that I could at last have a piece of my grandmother's wonderful cake. On this particular day, I saw him walking up the hill, about halfway up, but he wasn't alone.

There was another man I didn't recognize walking with him, holding his arm as they walked. You could see how happy they were, laughing and joking, and I rushed inside to tell Grandma that he was on his way and that he had someone with him. She wasn't best pleased at this news and came outside saying, "Who on earth is he bringing here today?"

But then she started telling me off, because he wasn't anywhere in sight and I oughtn't to tell lies. I tried to protest that I had seen him but no one believed me. About an hour later his friend, who I always called Uncle Jimmy, came to tell Grandma that Granddad had had a heart attack in the betting shop and had died.

Of course, this was a shock to everyone and I felt very strange about it. I really had seen my granddad walking up the hill that evening. Maybe the granddad I'd seen laughing with his friend was already dead and was being accompanied to heaven by an angel. Whoever it was, they looked very happy.

KEN
Madrid, Spain

I got lost in the mountains once. My car broke down on a high mountain road. It was very deserted up there and rather than wait for another car, which could have taken all day, I decided to walk down to the nearest village. This involved walking down the hill rather than following the road. But somehow I was going the wrong way, and after a few hours I realized I was completely lost. I'd been following the sun, but the direction I was going in was wrong and now I was hopelessly lost. It would be dark in a few hours and I was getting a bit worried.

At that point, I saw a white hawk hovering over me. It's a strange thing, but I felt like I had seen this bird before, when I was young, and always in difficult situations. Perhaps in dreams I had seen it. Now it seemed to be watching me. I decided to walk toward the bird, as I didn't have any other ideas. The bird kept moving on over the hills, and I kept following it. After about half an hour, I came to the ridge of a hill and there below me was the village. I'd been going in completely the wrong direction before I started following the hawk.

I don't know if that really was a guide, but it is interesting that the idea came into my head that I should follow it. It doesn't really make sense, unless the idea to follow it came from outside me somehow.

JOHN, 41
Georgia, USA

My spirit guide is an angel called Lua. I can tell when he's there, because an immense feeling of peace and happiness comes over me and the hairs on my arms stand up. Lua acts as a kind of teacher in my life. When I am unsure how to act, or need advice, he will be there and I can meditate on various problems with him. The advice he gives me comes straight into my mind from his.

Most of the big decisions in my life, about my work and my private life, have been made after talking to Lua. I think we all have angels that are there to help and protect us, but you have to open your mind to them to be able to receive communications from them.

FRAN, 50
Durban, South Africa

After my mother died, I found it hard to come to terms with her departure. To start with, I didn't want to clear up her room and possessions, but after about a week I decided I had to go and do it. On her mantelpiece was a china angel she had kept with her for many years. She called it her guardian angel and she used to believe firmly that we are watched over by angels. I wasn't so sure then. She also told me, many times, that her mother came back to her sometimes as an angel. I used to find the idea a little bit scary when I was young.

When I went into that room, I picked up the angel and thought about what my mother used to say, and this strange feeling came over me. There was a beautiful smell of flowers, honeysuckle or something similar, and it was as though the room was suddenly filled with the warmth of bright sunlight, even though nothing really changed outside.

I realized that my mother was there in the room with me, even though I couldn't see her. It was an eerie feeling—I was covered in goosebumps, and I looked around and said hello to her. I could feel her smiling when I did that. I realized that if I needed her, she would be there for me. I might not be able to speak with her, but just knowing she is there is a great help. When I feel down or sad,

I still pick up the angel and hold it in my hand, or I call out to my mother in my mind, and often the same thing happens. I know that she comes to me when I need her. I don't remember why I used to find the idea scary. Now I find it very comforting to know that the one person I could always count on is still there for me.

CARLA
South Carolina, USA

My older sister died when she was thirteen and I was nine. She got hit by a truck on her way home from school one afternoon. They said she died instantly. The truck was speeding and they later found out that the driver had been drinking. He had his license revoked for a while, but he's probably still out there driving now, despite having killed a young girl.

I'm convinced that she visits me as an angel whenever I get upset or stressed out about things. I missed not having a big sister to talk with about things. When I get upset, I tend to withdraw into myself and just feel bad rather than talk about it. There have been many times in my life—splitting up with boyfriends, college exams, my recent divorce—when I have felt bad and curled up on my own. After a while, something happens and I start to feel calmer. It's like I suddenly begin to believe I can cope. I know what I have to do to get back on track.

It always starts with this warm, comforting feeling coming over me and I feel less stressed. It's almost as if someone is holding my hand. I'm sure that someone is my sister and she's become some sort of angel who protects me like my guardian angel. I think she does it because she's my big sister and she never got the chance to do those things in real life, so she has returned as an angel to protect me. I feel so happy that she does.

DERRICK
Melbourne, Australia

I never knew my grandfather because he died just before I was born. My mum always used to tell me what a lovely man he was and how he would have loved me had he met me.

When I was about five years old, my mum, dad, and brothers were in the kitchen getting lunch ready and I was in the living room, sitting on the floor watching TV.

I turned around suddenly and there was a man sitting on the sofa behind me. He was wearing a brown suit and was quite old, with white hair. He told me that he loved me and would always look after me. My mum poked her head round the door and asked me who was I talking to.

When I looked at the sofa it was empty. The man had gone. I asked my mum where he had gone, and she seemed puzzled and a bit anxious; she told me there was no one else at home. When I went into the dining room to have lunch, I saw the man again, in a photograph on the piano. Mum said it was my grandfather, her dad. I have never seen him since, though I still like to think that he's my guardian angel, and I often talk to him about things when life gets a bit rough.

SARAH
Liverpool, England

I'm sure I saw an angel when I was a little girl. My grandmother had died and she'd been laid out in her coffin in the front parlor. That's what they did in those days, so that people could come and pay their respects. I'd never seen a dead body before, so I was half scared to death and half fascinated. I first went in with my mum and held her hand while I said my goodbyes. Later that night, while everyone was in the kitchen talking, I crept downstairs again and sneaked into the parlor.

There was a woman standing next to her coffin. She didn't look like anyone who lived near us. I certainly hadn't ever seen her before. There was a kind of glow around her; it was beautiful and made her look like something from another world. I watched from the door for a while, then she turned and smiled at me. And I knew, I just knew that she was an angel and that she'd come for my grandmother. I've always been so glad to have seen her. My grandmother was very special.

GERTRUDE
Berlin, Germany

When I was a little girl, I was terrified of the dark. I hated waking up in the dark. Sometimes when I did wake up, there was an old man sitting by my bed, talking to me quietly and smiling at me kindly. I could never hear what he was saying, but I could tell he meant well and so it was comforting.

I told my mother about this after I became a teenager. She asked me to describe him. When I did, she started to cry and told me that it was my grandfather, her father, who had died shortly before I was born. When she showed me a photograph of him, I was startled because it really was the same man.

My mother said he loved to make up stories, and that when she had been a little girl, he would often sit by her bed at night, telling her the stories he made up. That must have been what he was doing for me, too. Even though I couldn't hear them, it made me feel happy that he came back to tell them to me.

Boris
Cornwall, England

My mother had this little terrier dog, Ben, which she loved so much. She had even left instructions on how to look after him should anything happen to her. She died suddenly in a car accident in 2002, and I followed her wishes and brought the dog to live with me. I remember going into the kitchen, a year to the very day that Mum was killed, and seeing Ben just sitting on the kitchen floor wagging his tail, looking so happy. In front of him, there seemed to be this kind of glow. It vanished almost immediately when I saw it. I think it was my mum, just checking on her beloved little dog. The experience left behind a kind of peaceful feeling and I've known since that my mum is happy with how I'm looking after her dog.

JOHN
New York, USA

After my dad died when I was at college, I went through quite a bad time. I'd never really got along with him and felt that we'd never taken time to settle our differences before he died. He was disappointed that I'd chosen to study art history rather than medicine or law, and I felt he just wanted to show off to the neighbors about his "professional" son. Anyway, he died suddenly of a heart attack when he was fifty and it caught me completely off guard.

One day I was just lying on my bed, listening to music, when I felt really cold and the hairs on my arms stood on end. It felt like someone was sitting there holding my hand. I knew at that moment that it was all right, that my dad understood and that our differences could finally be put to rest. After that day, I got on with my studies and became much happier again.

SHERI, 35
New York, USA

Whenever I thought of angels when I was small, I pictured them the way everybody seems to—tall and glowing with wings and a halo—but now I think that they can appear exactly as they wish and in whatever way suits their purpose. My angel was a big black Labrador with a worn leather collar, which had a disc attached that said "Jack" and an address on the other side of town.

I'd been working at a small family-run Italian restaurant to help pay my way through college and, although there wasn't much money and the tips only just kept me alive, I enjoyed the time I spent there. The owner swore that he made the best *spaghetti all'aglio e olio* (that's pasta with oil and garlic to you) outside Naples. And he might just have been right; it tasted really good.

But he wasn't such a nice guy in other ways, and one night he came on to me in the kitchen while his wife was with some customers out front. Can you believe that? She was right there in the building. I walked out the back door and never came back. But it was a really bad time for me for something like that to have happened and I didn't know what I was going to do without the money, however bad the situation was.

I went back to my apartment and sat down to try and figure out how I was going to make that month's rent, then just gave up and got in my car. I drove up to a place on the edge of the woods that has a picnic area, and I sat down and looked at the sunset. It was late summer and even though it was only about eight in the evening, there was no one there but me.

After I'd been there for a while, I noticed a big old black Labrador nosing his way through the litter near the parking area. After a bit he made his way over to where I was sitting on the grass and sat down right next to me. I've never had a dog so I was a little nervous, but he seemed so calm and nice that I stretched out my hand and rubbed his head. He leaned into my shoulder and seemed to like the attention that he was getting from me. I felt a warmth and companionship from him that I'd never gotten from another human being. That's when I looked at his nametag. "Hi, Jack," I said, "you want to sit for a while?"

That's what we did, me stroking his head and him leaning on me, and a real peace came over me. I didn't exactly forget the trouble I'd had in the restaurant and the way I'd been treated, but it seemed to fade away into the sunset. I knew I'd be all right. I don't know how long we sat there—it can't have been more than fifteen minutes—before I saw a woman over on the other side of the picnic area. She had white hair and was dressed in a jogging suit and looked to be maybe fifty or so.

She waved at me and Jack and smiled, then my Labrador friend got up and ran over to her. She waved again and pointed at my car. I looked, of course, and when I turned back she had gone and so had the dog. The thing is, there wasn't another car around, and I couldn't see where she might have come from.

I got back in my car and drove home feeling completely different from the way I'd been on the way up there. I checked the address that I'd remembered from Jack's tag but it didn't seem to make sense as a real address. But I still felt better than I ever had and I still thought, even after my bad night, that things would work out and that college would be okay, which it was.

At this point, I don't know who was the angel: Jack or his owner—whom I never could find, but who I believe was sent to look after me on a not-so-nice evening and who left me feeling better than I ever had. Maybe it was both of them. That seems about right to me.

ADELE, 30
Illinois, USA

I was at the wedding of my closest friend. They held it outside at her parents' house on a lovely Saturday in June. It was beautiful weather. I was really happy because the man my friend was marrying was exactly right for her. I've always liked her family, and there were a lot of people there that I was happy to see. It was just one of those wonderful days when everything comes together and you can't express how happy you are.

As the bride and groom were about to say their vows, I saw three white birds fly down over their heads and settle on a tree, which was behind the minister. They sat there very attentively, watching the people at the wedding. You know the way birds cock their heads. I noticed them because white birds are not that common here, so I was wondering what kind of bird they could possibly be.

I looked back up at them a few times as the service continued and still they were watching. Then, just as my friend said "I do" and her new husband put the ring on her finger, the three birds rose up as one and flew straight over us all. I've told my friend that her wedding was blessed by angels. She's the happiest bride ever, anyway, but it never does any harm to have some extra help, does it?

OTHER ANGELIC
ENCOUNTERS

It's hard to clearly categorize every angelic encounter. This chapter is composed of various stories that I found interesting, but which didn't quite fit in with any of the other chapters. Some accounts I've included because the people who sent them to me truly believed their experiences were related to angels. Near-death experiences in particular seem to merit an entire book of their own. The accounts of near-death experiences that I have included here were selected because they involved angels or the awareness of angels.

JANEY, 43
Maryland, USA

I had a motorcycle crash a few years ago. A car came out of a side road without even looking and crashed into the side of me. I went over the edge of the road, over the pavement, and into a wall, at which point I came off the bike and was catapulted into a field. I hit my head pretty badly and did myself plenty of damage, too. The driver did at least stop and make sure that someone called 911; in fact, I think he felt pretty bad about it.

Anyway, I was knocked out cold, and then woke up on a gurney being pushed down a corridor in a hospital somewhere. I was in terrible pain and everything was distorted and weird. I saw that terrible white light over me. I knew immediately that I was dying and that I had to go to the light. But I didn't want to go.

I was rising up above my body. For a moment the pain stopped and I could see myself on this gurney, with doctors all around me. They had all kinds of instruments attached to me, and someone was holding my head and shouting. At that moment, I actually felt calm, because I knew that this way the pain wouldn't start again. Then I remembered my boyfriend and my family, and I didn't want to go.

There was an angel there then. I don't know when she arrived, but she was beside me, looking down. All she said was, "You can go back if you want." I think we both knew there wasn't time to think about it. I had to either let go and keep going, or go back. I decided to go back and then I was there again, on the gurney, looking up, in all the same pain. It took me a while to recuperate, but the doctors said I'd nearly died, and I know for sure that they were right.

HEIKE
Munich, Germany

I see heaven sometimes when I am half asleep. I'm not sure why. It's not a dream I have at nighttime. But sometimes in the afternoon or in the morning I might be sitting in a chair, feeling a bit tired, and I will start to doze off, and that's when I see it.

Perhaps it's because a lot of people I know have died. My brother died of cancer when he was young, and my mother killed herself a few years ago. Three of my friends have died in the last ten years as well—one of a drug overdose, one in an accident, and one from anorexia. I am no stranger to the dead in any case.

It is like a beautiful warm light comes over me. People think that death must be a cold, bad place, but I realize that it is simply a better place. In the light I can make out faces, but it is not the people I know who have died. It is the faces of angels who are coming to greet me.

There is a beautiful music I hear. It is full of the most beautiful harmonies and cadences. I am a musician and I have tried many times to write down what I hear, but it is beyond human comprehension. It is as though there are notes that you have never heard before that harmonize more perfectly than anything you have ever imagined. If you can imagine seeing a completely new color, different from anything you have ever seen, that is what it sounds like. So there is this beautiful music and the angels come out to meet me, and I know that the people I know who have died are there, but I can't see them. I can't see them unless I die too, and I don't want to die.

When the music stops and I am back in the light of a normal day, I always feel very cold and a little bit sad. I have to go and sit in front of the heater with it turned up as high as possible to try to stay warm. It is as though I remember the warmth of heaven and can't deal with the normal temperature of the day around me. Then the moment passes and I warm up and I just feel glad that I have been allowed this glimpse of something else, something that I will not be able to really experience until after I die.

ANTHONY, 29
South Carolina, USA

I recently had an operation. It was just a routine one to remove a small growth, but I had to be unconscious, so they gave me a general anesthetic. As I was started to go under, I looked around, and standing behind all the doctors and nurses who were around me, I could see bright shining lights and the faces of angels watching me. It was very clear and distinct.

When I woke up after the operation, I saw them again, just for a moment. They were exactly how you would imagine angels to look—bright, shining white light and beautiful human forms. Their eyes were silver or gold and they had very beautiful faces.

JOHN, 21
Nevada, USA

Sometimes I wake up in the night and there are two angels standing at the end of my bed and two standing above my head. I remember a nursery rhyme book from when I was small. I don't remember the exact rhyme, but I remember the picture, which was of four angels in this arrangement. It was a dark blue and black picture, quite somber, and the angels were actually bears—it was a book for small children. I know that it must have made a deep impression on me, because I remember that picture but I don't remember much else about the book.

When the angels are there around my bed, I know that each of them has a particular role in my life. I can't exactly say what those roles are, but I know they are there for a reason. They're not bears, of course. They are like people but I don't really see their faces. I see them standing there, but their faces are too high above me to be seen. I see their white wings, glistening in the light.

It's not an entirely comfortable dream (if it is a dream). I feel I they may be judging me, and no matter how hard we try, there are always things in our life of which we are ashamed or uncertain. But I don't feel they are judging me too harshly. They are noting my sins without condemning me for them.

Perhaps none of this really means anything, but it is a very vivid vision and something that makes me view life differently the next day. If angels are there recording my actions in some way, then surely it adds a greater weight to what I do. I think about it when I walk past a homeless person, or when I get angry at people around me for silly reasons. I won't swear that it always makes me a better person, but perhaps it makes me more conscious of my faults.

CALLY, 65
Iowa, USA

I was with my mother when she died. She had been ill for quite some time, so it was not a great surprise to us. In fact, she had outdone the doctors, who kept giving us warnings that she might not last much longer, but she kept on going and giving the lie to their warnings. She amazed everyone with her fortitude and cheerful attitude toward the illness. I only hope that I have half the spirit to deal with adversity that she showed in her last months.

The day she died was one of the few days I remember her saying anything less than positive. She told me she was feeling a bit weak and that wasn't sure she was going to be there much longer. She told me not to worry if she died, and that she had left her will and instructions in the hall table. Of course, she had told me this before and I told her what I always did, that she was going to be around longer than me. But I was worried. I wanted to call the doctors, but she said they didn't know what they were doing and she couldn't be bothered with them.

My brother was there with me that night, after he came from work, and we sat with our mother upstairs, watching a film on the television. Then we took turns reading to her from the book she had been reading. She didn't like reading herself as it tired her, but she enjoyed having us read to her. I was happy to be able to do this for her when she had spent so long reading to me and teaching me to read when I was little.

We finished the chapter and asked if she wanted another one, but she said no, she wanted to lie still for a while. We stayed with her, talking quietly, expecting her to fall asleep. Then she pointed up and said, "Look." We looked and there was nothing there, so we asked what she was pointing at.

"Can't you see them? The angels?" she said. We told her we couldn't. Then she said, "No, I suppose you can't. Just me. But they're so lovely. I wish you could see them."

She just lay there, staring up at them with a beautiful, calm expression on her face. My brother and I looked at each other, but he shrugged and we didn't want to talk in case we interrupted her reverie. Then she died. She just breathed out and didn't breathe back in again. It was that simple. We didn't try to revive her, because both of us knew that it was natural, and that she was dying in any case. In retrospect, I'm just happy that I was able to be there when she went, and also that she died looking so happy.

SAKUMI, 37
Tokyo, Japan

I was brought up believing in ghosts; I saw them often. In Japan it is believed that the spirits of your ancestors stay with you, and I often saw my grandparents after they died. Perhaps if you believe, you can see them more easily when they come to visit. They would come and visit me in my bedroom, and once I saw them in the park. Once or twice I saw ghosts of people I didn't know, strangers in the street, or perhaps someone who had lived in our house a long time ago. I saw someone walking up the stairs when the house was empty when I was a teenager. None of this scared me; it just seemed normal.

Just once, I had an experience that was quite different. A friend of mine was hit by a car and she was in the hospital, in critical condition. I went to visit her a lot. She was in a coma for two days and no one was sure if she would survive. I was about twenty and I took my turn sitting with her, talking to her, to try and bring her back.

About one in the morning, I was the only one there with her, as her parents had gone home. I heard a terrible rushing noise and the room became white with light, and there were two giant figures standing at the bottom of her bed. They were about eight feet tall and very stern. I was frozen with fear in my chair, but they completely ignored me. They were there a while—it could have been a minute or ten minutes, I couldn't tell.

Then there was the rushing sound again and they were gone. I had no idea what had happened. Perhaps my friend was close to death at that moment and they came to observe or help. They weren't there for me, so there was no need for me to know anything. They definitely weren't ghosts, so I believe they were a completely different kind of spiritual being.

I have noticed since I came to live in America that people don't believe in ghosts so easily. They find it quite strange when I talk about my grandparents, so I tend not to speak of these things. But the figures I saw in the hospital that night seem to me to be more like angels than ghosts. I haven't seen anything like it since, and I would be quite terrified if I ever did again, but it is not fear because they mean any harm. It is just awe of something that is beyond anything that I can possibly comprehend.

ISAAC, 20
New York, USA

I often see angels when I am on the edge of sleep. Just as I am about to fall asleep or just as I am waking up, I look around and see one or two angels in the room. Sometimes they are sitting in the chairs in the corner of the room. Sometimes they are standing next to the bed. They are looking at me and they have kind faces. There is one in particular that I often see, who has gray hair and a very rugged face. Perhaps he is my guardian angel.

I smile when I see them and they smile back, but it is at that half-awake moment when it is hard to speak. Then I either fall asleep, happy that they are there, or I wake up properly and they are gone. I think that there is a kind of altered state where you can see aspects of reality that would otherwise be hidden from you, and that's what happens to me on the edge of sleep.

ALAN, 38
London, England

I don't really know if I met a real angel or not, but I like to think I did. My wife and I visited Milan a couple years ago. It was one of those cheap flights that you can book on the Internet. We decided one weekend that we deserved a few days away and the next weekend we were there. We walked around and looked at the cathedral, which is huge, and the arcade that leads onto the cathedral piazza, and had a very nice time.

We wanted to see Da Vinci's *The Last Supper*, but the queues were too long and it was staggeringly hot, so we went to a café and had some cold drinks instead. The only other place that we wanted to see never seemed to be open, but we thought it was worth one more visit, just to check. It was an ossuary, which is, at least in Milan, a chapel where all the inside decoration is made out of people's bones.

It sounds a bit gruesome, but I'd read about it somewhere and I really wanted to see what it was like. The bones, apparently, had come from an old graveyard that had been dug up in the seventeenth century to make way for another church, and had all been taken to this existing chapel for safekeeping. I can't remember the name of it, and I can't find my guidebook, but if you ever go, it's just behind the big cathedral, down a little side road.

As I said, we'd tried to get in several times before and failed, but the sign on the front had said it was open this afternoon at three o'clock. It was just after that, so we went to have one more try. But when we got there, it was closed again. We were just about to leave when a very small, very old man came from nowhere, seemingly, and spoke to us in Italian.

I didn't understand, but it gradually became clear that he had the keys and that he'd be very pleased to let us in. Well, it was just beautiful and not gruesome at all. It was completely decorated with the bones of long-dead people, but they were arranged in patterns and crucifixes and stretched from the floor to the highest point of the walls.

The little Italian man stayed with us long enough to tell us to look at what he called "the angles in the sky." The "angles" turned out to be a fabulously painted, domed ceiling to the chapel, which showed a vast array of angels, all in golden clothing with wings, shimmering in a deep blue sky. The only other thing he said was that the people whose bones were at the top of all the walls were lucky because they were closer to the "angles in the sky," and that the "angles" were the luckiest of all because they were the closest to heaven. He was a lovely man.

When we had spent a long time in that wonderful building, I looked for him to thank him for appearing just when we were about to give up, but he'd gone. I like to think that he, too, was an "angle." He certainly seemed to be close to heaven.

MARTIN
Vermont, USA

When we were teenagers, we used to love playing in the snow in the winter. We used to slide down hills on pieces of wood or tin trays stolen from our houses. Late one winter afternoon, we were about to have our final "sleigh" ride when this white, glowing light appeared, glinting on the snow.

We all stopped in our tracks and just stared at the glowing snow. We weren't afraid or anything. Even though the light was strange like nothing we'd ever seen before, it felt kindly and warm. It was like a glowing and friendly warmth. It warmed all of us, then just disappeared as quickly and mysteriously as it had appeared.

We checked the newspaper and the TV news in the following days but there was no mention of any "lights in the sky" or anything. I'm convinced it was an angel, because it made us all feel so cozy and warm and safe. That's how an angel should make you feel.

Sean, 27
Maryland, USA

I was in the local park on New Year's Day last year. I have to tell you, I'd been behaving pretty atrociously. Over Christmas, after a party, I'd been unfaithful to my long-term girlfriend—just a casual, stupid thing, but I knew that she would be really upset if I told her. And I didn't know if I should tell her or what to do. I mean, was it just selfish to tell her, to get the guilt off my chest? Or was it even worse to try to keep it secret? And while I'd been worrying about all this, I'd been drinking too much and had a big drunken fight with my roommate, so he wasn't talking to me. Everything seemed bad and I knew it was my fault, no excuses.

So I was in the park, looking at the geese on the pond, just walking around trying to think things through, very anxious and upset, not really facing up to things. It was really cold and misty, so cold your breath was in clouds around you. And then I felt this breath on my face, like someone very warm was breathing right up close to me. And there was a hand on my shoulder. There was no one there but I really did feel it. What it was like was someone who couldn't help, because there was nothing that could make the situation right, but the most they could do was let me know that they were there for me. Like a really close friend might do if you've totally screwed up (if you're lucky). But it was more than that, too. I felt myself calm right down, all the way through me. I got warmer and less agitated. I started to think straight; instead of looking for people to blame, I started to think about exactly what had happened and why.

I was pretty sure it was an angel who helped me face up to things there. They couldn't fix it all for me, but I did try my best to honestly face up to my own mistakes after that. I apologized to my roommate, and even though I ended up splitting up with the girl, I was straight with her and let her know exactly how I felt. How I see it is this: you can't avoid making mistakes in life, but sometimes you need a bit of help in being strong enough to admit to them and work out where to go next.

LUKE, 34
Wales

I used to play guitar in a band. We were on stage one day at a sound check when the bassist got electrocuted. Basically his amplifier was short-circuiting and, when he put one hand on the bass strings and one on the microphone, he was completing a circuit, and the current went through him.

For a moment we didn't know what had happened. He gave a kind of strangled shout and then he was falling about on the stage. For a moment we just thought he was messing about, but he hit the singer, and for a moment he got a shock too. The singer started shouting "Plugs!" and we all got the message. I pulled one set of plugs out of the wall—the wrong ones. But luckily the keyboard player found the right one and yanked it out.

The whole thing only took about five to ten seconds, but it all seemed to happen in slow motion. Afterward the bass player had a burned patch on his finger where it had been in contact with the strings, and his heart was quite jumpy. We cancelled the gig; there was nothing else for it. We wanted him to go to the hospital for a check-up; electricity can do strange things to you that you don't realize. But he refused. He just wanted to go outside and sit down. In fact, he'd have played the gig even, but his gear was too dangerous to use again, and we were all shaken up by it. It would have been stupid to take the risk.

I went out to talk to him about it, meaning to have one more go at getting him to go to the emergency room.

It was a mild, sunny evening and we sat on this wall outside the bar where the gig was supposed to be. He was looking all round him as though things looked strange.

I asked him if he was okay, and he told me that while he had been being electrocuted, he had seen angels all around him. I said it sounded like a hallucination, or did he think he was going to die? He said no, that hadn't even crossed his mind. It was like the illusion we see every day had fallen away and he had realized that there were angels all around us, standing there, talking to each other, watching us. They had stopped to watch him, and he had still been able to see them after we switched the current off, smiling at him now that he was okay. But then they had slowly faded.

He said that was why he had been so impatient with us when we were talking about the hospital and all that. It was like we were breaking the spell and all the while this vision he'd had of the angels around us was fading, until he couldn't see them at all. Now he wanted to just walk home quietly while it was still fresh in his mind. And he set off, in the wrong direction, to walk home, still looking all around him.

I've always remembered that image—the idea that behind what we see, there is actually another reality where the angels are just going about their business and keeping an eye on what happens in our world. I'm not sure if it was a hallucination on his part or real, but there is something very appealing about the thought, anyway.

SUSAN

Cape Town, South Africa

My grandmother had a stroke when she was seventy-nine. It made her paralyzed from the waist down and we'd had to put her in a nursing home because she could no longer look after herself. It upset the whole family to have to do this, but we knew we had no choice. Our homes were not adapted for wheelchairs and my mother, father, and brother all have full-time jobs, as do I.

She was unhappy after the stroke. She had always loved gardening and walking, just being outdoors, really. Whenever we visited, and someone visited every day, she was up and down in terms of her mood. She often got very depressed and it was distressing to see someone you loved being so down.

She died after being in the home nearly two years. I was the first person the staff contacted and I went straight there. When I went into my grandmother's room, she was lying on the bed and all around her there seemed to be this glowing light. I stood back and watched as it gradually faded. It wasn't frightening; I'd say it was more comforting than anything else. I went over to my grandmother's bedside and she had a smile on her face. It was lovely to see that after seeing her so depressed. Even though we were all tremendously upset after her death, I think the light was the angels taking her soul to heaven.

AFTERWORD

It's impossible for us to know in our normal lives what heaven or the afterlife might be like, but we can have direct knowledge of angels. Because angels are able to cross between the physical world and the world of pure spirit, they may be the most direct experience we can have of the sphere of divinity.

It seems clear that humans often need a helping hand. We can be weak, cruel, unaware, and selfish. But also, with or without a helping hand, we can be brave, kind, and selfless. Perhaps this is why the angels love us enough to intervene or to bring us messages. They see our faults, but they also see our potential. I think they love children best of all, because children are innocent of the sins and weaknesses that afflict us in later life. But it seems that angels are also willing to give even the weakest of us a second chance. Sometimes they save us when we don't seem to deserve saving; other times they show us the way out of the problems we have created for ourselves.

In many of the stories recounted here, the humanity and decency of ordinary human beings in extraordinary situations shines through strongly, like the drug addict or petty criminal who musters the strength to realize his sins and turn his life around, or people who have lost their loved ones and have had to face up to their own faults in reacting to these tragedies, or those who have shown bravery in the face of violence, evil, or misfortune. From all of these accounts we can draw strength and a renewed faith in our fellow residents of planet Earth.

The fact that people believe in angels also seems to be an expression of our essential goodness. We have enough comprehension of good and evil to recognize goodness in all situations. People are, sadly, not always able to stay on the path of goodness, and they stray into weak or evil acts. But it is that spark of goodness with which we are born that can always lead us back into the light. Angels can always see that spark of goodness, and for that reason, our connection to angels is of the greatest importance in our everyday lives.

I have always believed in angels, but now I feel their presence on a daily basis. I have heard and seen enough to convince me that they are always with us, and I don't need any overt signs or messages from them to believe that they are here to watch over us. I like to think that belief gives me even more reason to live my life in a way that would please the angels. I hope that you have found this book an inspiration. It has been a great pleasure to compile it, and I am grateful for the opportunity to act as an intermediary and bring you these accounts.

Angels are with us, whether we believe in them or not. But the more we believe in them, the more likely we are to recognize them when we encounter them. I hope and trust that the next time an angel crosses your path, you will recognize that beautiful being and be open to the angels' positive influence in your life.